Pitt Series in Policy and
Institutional Studies

Extraordinary Measures

The Exercise of Prerogative Powers in the United States

Daniel P. Franklin

University of Pittsburgh Press

Published by the University of Pittsburgh Press, Pittsburgh, Pa., 15260
Copyright © 1991, University of Pittsburgh Press
Baker and Taylor International, London
Manufactured in the United States of America

Library of Congress Cataloging-in-Publication Data

Franklin, Daniel P.
    Extraordinary measures : the exercise of prerogative powers in the
United States / Daniel P. Franklin.
        p.   cm. — (Pitt series in policy and institutional studies)
    Includes index.
    ISBN 0-8229-3672-0. — ISBN 0-8229-5451-6 (pbk.)
    1. War and emergency powers—United States.   2. Implied powers
(Constitutional law)—United States.   I. Title.   II. Series.
JK339.F73   1991
320.4'04'0973—dc20   90-21078
                                                                CIP

Contents

Extraordinary
Measures

1 Toward a Comprehensive Theory of Prerogative in American Politics

On occasion it becomes necessary for a democratic government to act without the express permission of its citizens or even all of its elected officials. Extraordinary events may create unique situations for which there are no explicit constitutional grants, public laws, or legal precedents. It is at these times that the principles of self-government are sorely tested. For it is at these times that a government must act beyond formal constitutional control for the public good or even for the sake of survival. Clearly, extraordinary powers can be abused to the detriment of liberties and civil rights; yet, necessity dictates the exercise of emergency powers, at times, in any republic. This fact creates a critical problem for liberal, republican theorists. How can plenary power be reconciled with democratic principles, and how can citizens be protected against governmental abuse of authority in times of emergency?

The United States government, I will argue, is fully capable of protecting itself in times of emergency within the confines of the Constitution. In order to make this argument, I shall advance an expanded notion of constitutionalism. The Constitution is both a construct and a concept. Beyond the limits of the written constitution exist certain authorities that accrue to all states. It is the prerogative of governments to take extraordinary actions for the protection of the state. These extraordinary or "prerogative" powers may exist outside the written constitution, but this is not to say that governmental action in defense of the nation is without limits. Law without limits is a contradiction in terms. Rather,

3

there exists at a different, deeper level of the Constitution provision for and limits on the exercise of prerogative powers. When exercised properly, prerogative powers are thoroughly constitutional.

The limits and exercise of prerogative powers have long been a point of contention. In medieval Europe the exercise of emergency powers was the prerogative of the king. According to medieval law, prerogative powers were not so much a distinct set of authorities as they were the privilege of position. In its most extreme interpretation, the prerogative of the crown was considered to be absolute. The royal prerogative, therefore, did not describe the power of the king so much as it defined the supremacy of the king in government. As the formal, governing role of the king eroded, however, the prerogatives of the crown were transferred.

For those subjects in prerevolutionary England who believed in the supremacy of the monarch (as opposed to the supremacy of law), it was the prerogative of the king ultimately to exercise any authority he saw fit. Accordingly, even unjust or unwise edicts issued by the king were to be obeyed by the community. However, for those who believed in the supremacy and the antecedence of law, prerogative powers existed as a set of authorities distinct from the king's person.[1] For the king's subjects in the American colonies who strained at the royal tether, the royal prerogative could "only be exerted while in the Hands of the best and most benign sovereign, for the Good of his People, and not for their Destruction."[2] Unlawful or harmful exercises of prerogative by the king were to be resisted or ignored. For others, particularly those who were left behind in England, prerogative powers could be parceled out in their particulars to the different estates as represented in government. Even so, the English Constitution imposed certain restraints on the action of Parliament.[3] Consequently, as the belief in the supremacy of law became ascendant throughout the seventeenth and eighteenth centuries, it became more accurate to describe prerogatives as a distinct set of powers that emanated from the state rather than from the person of the ruler.

This definitional shift has never been clearly registered in American social science. Modern legal analysts still use the term *prerogative* to describe both the powers of position and powers of the state. For example, *Black's Law Dictionary* defines prerogative as:

An exclusive or peculiar right or privilege. The special power, privilege, immunity, right or advantage vested in an official person, either generally, or in respect to the things of his office, or in an official body, as a court or legislature.[4]

There is a clear precedent for this kind of definition. For example, John Locke defined prerogative power as:

A power, in the hands of the prince, to provide for the public good in cases, which depending upon unforeseen and uncertain occurrences, certain and unalterable laws could not safely direct; whatsoever shall be done manifestly for the good of the people, and the establishing the government upon its true foundations, is, and always will be just prerogative.[5]

But is this definition an accurate foundation upon which to ground our current concept of prerogative powers?

In particular, it is customary for modern American political analysts to focus on the presidential prerogative to the exclusion of the powers of other branches of government.[6] This emphasis on the presidential prerogative is almost certainly a function of the agenda set by past presidents who sometimes made extravagant claims to executive entitlements.[7] But does this mean that the president, as chief executive, exercises certain powers that naturally or constitutionally emanate from his position in government? Or is it more accurate to define the prerogative powers of the president as those powers that accrue to the state that are exercised in a special way or under a special set of circumstances by the president?

The second approach is more plausible. To suggest that a certain set of prerogatives emanate exclusively from the presidency is to deny the principles of shared power in American government. Powers are shared in American government to the extent that Congress, if it so desires, can interfere with the exercise of presidential prerogatives. Appropriations can be cut, vetoes can be overridden, lawsuits can be filed, opposition candidacies can be inspired, and investigations can be mounted all in opposition to the exercise of the "president's prerogatives." Rather, the president's *position* in the decision-making scheme furnishes the chief executive with certain advantages in the exercise of prerogative powers. The prerogatives of government in the United States are in reality vested in the collective. Therefore, when we talk about prerogative powers as exercised by the president *or* Congress *or* the courts, we talk about institutions of government as responsible for the exercise of, and not the original source of, prerogative powers. Prerogative powers in the American context, therefore, are a set of powers emanating from the state.

Every state, democratic or authoritarian, will be forced to respond to emergencies with extraordinary measures. As Franz Neumann wrote:

No society in recorded history has ever been able to dispense with political power. This is as true of liberalism as of absolutism, as true of laissez faire as of an interventionist state. No greater disservice has been rendered to political science than the statement that the liberal state was a "weak" state. It was precisely as strong as it needed to be in the circumstances. It acquired substantial colonial empires, waged wars, held down internal disorders, and stabilized itself over long periods of time.[8]

In practice, prerogatives in the United States may be exercised to the exclusion of the written constitution. Prerogatives are exercised for "reasons of state," the primary, but not exclusive, pursuit of which is national survival. Desperate times have called for desperate measures in the United States. As we shall see, many of the "desperate measures" sanctioned by the American government have gone well beyond the Bill of Rights.

The legitimation of powers exercised beyond the Constitution calls into question the meaning of constitutionalism in the American context. Are prerogative powers constitutional? If so, it must be assumed that the written constitution has been supplanted in practice by a "living" constitution that permits the exercise of prerogative powers to the detriment of individual rights. If not, the alternative view may be that, particularly (but not exclusively) in times of emergency, we live in a lawless state.

Subjects of a monarch could trust in God, for whom the king was an agent, that the prerogative powers of his government would not be abused. In a republic, prerogative powers are not so clearly vested and, therefore, not so easily controlled. Because it is inescapable that the people's representatives must have some leeway to act in case of emergency, prerogative powers present five separate problems for republican thinkers. First, there is the problem of deciding just what situation qualifies as dangerous or significant enough to require the exercise of a prerogative. Second, there is the problem of accountability. How are persons or institutions in a democratic government to be held accountable for their actions? Third, in a problem special to American democracy (a system constructed according to the principle of the separation of powers), it is important to decide which of the representative institutions should be allowed to exercise prerogative powers and at what stage and in what type of crisis different institutions should be involved. Fourth, even if the constitution of a state does not provide an explicit guide, civil libertarians have to decide how far a government can go in protecting itself. After all, for some, the sacrifice of liberty for the sake of national survival represents, in effect, the loss of security itself. Finally, even if we can agree that there exists a distinct set of prerogative powers in government, there is an inherent resistance in the American philosophical and legal tradition to the notion that certain powers can be exercised, for whatever purpose, beyond restraint.

There are a broad variety of situations in which the exercise of prerogative powers may be necessary. In times of war, insurrection, in the exercise of diplomacy or in executing the law when time constraints are involved, circumstance dictates the use of plenary powers. It is important to note that prerogative powers are not exercised exclusively in foreign affairs or even in pursuit of national survival. The courts have sanctioned the exercise of prerogative powers that are, at most, only very loosely related to national survival. For example, in the day-to-day workings of government novel situations will produce obstacles or opportunities to which government officials must respond quickly, without consulting others, or lose the initiative.

In American government one of the most frequent exercises of prerogative powers in peacetime occurs in the president's use of impoundments. While the executive branch may be directed by the law and the Constitution to spend funds appropriated by Congress, it has long been a principle recognized in statute that the president may impound funds at his own discretion in order to effect savings or promote efficiency.[9] Even though impoundment powers are recognized in statute, they are still prerogatives (or extraconstitutional) to the extent that Congress cannot legally delegate away its appropriations power. Presumably, there are some constitutional arrangements that can never be altered. Impoundment authority, therefore, exists in legal limbo somewhere between what is practical and what is strictly constitutional.

The exercise of plenary powers in situations in which national survival is not at stake compounds the problem of defining prerogative. Artificial distinctions that are made between foreign and domestic policy do not necessarily delineate or differentiate between the circumstances in which prerogatives may properly be applied. Rather, the exercise of prerogative is a function of circumstance, not of law. Emergencies can never be anticipated in all their manifestations.[10] This fact confounds constitutional principles in a state dedicated to the rule of "law not men."

Practical considerations such as time constraints or security concerns dictate that the prerogative power in the United States be wielded primarily by the executive branch. But how is the president to be held to account for decisions made in the absence of the concurrence of the coordinate branches of government? This is to say that the legislative and judicial branches act as conduits of prerogative powers as well. No one challenges the right of the president to defend the nation against foreign attack. However, the vast majority of emergency decisions are not so clear-cut.[11] Because decisions concerning the war power or diplomacy have the effect of legislation, Congress, if at all possible, should be consulted in advance of making far-reaching national commitments. Nevertheless, the meaning of "appropriate" consultation between the executive and legislative branches in case of emergency has never been well established.[12] Consequently, situations that require the exercise of extraordinary powers are the focus of great constitutional debates in the United States.

To adjudicate these disputes, the courts also play an important role in ensuring the accountability of the executive. However, in order to sustain a theory of constitutionality that is commensurate with the exercise of prerogative powers, we must view the Constitution as being a document of some flexibility. This presents a difficulty for the courts in the adjudication of disputes. A flexible constitution often fails to provide objective standards for the settlement of claims. As one constitutional scholar explained: "Sovereign power is by definition absolute. Yet since sovereign power is also by definition legitimate power, the use of power in arbitrary or illegitimate ways divests it of the quality of sovereignty. One of the biggest obstacles to our understanding of the political theory of the American Revolution has been the tendency to confuse absolute with arbitrary power."[13] Consequently, American jurists face almost insurmountable difficulties in agreeing on the limits of sovereignty in connection with the exercise of prerogative power.

By and large, the courts interpret disputes between the branches as "political questions" that are beyond the scope of judicial review. As Justice Marshall commented in Marbury v. Madison, the president is vested "with certain important political powers, in the exercise of which he is to use his own discretion, and is accountable only to his country in his political character, and to his own conscience."[14] However, in that same decision, Marshall went beyond the previously accepted limits of the Court's authority to suggest that the federal judiciary not only had the right to review the actions of states (an authority that was generally recognized), but also the power to review and determine the constitutionality of acts of Congress and the president. In the nineteenth century the Court used this power of judicial review sparingly, particularly prior to the Civil War. However, especially in the last fifty years, the courts have established a significant amount of case law and precedent to the effect that there are certain acceptable, court-sanctioned (and consequently "legal") patterns in the exercise of prerogative powers. The exercise of prerogative powers, therefore, can be defined and delimited according to an identifiable, historical consensus and practice.

Nevertheless, it has never been entirely clear what the absolute limits to the exercise of prerogative powers are in case of emergencies. Supposedly, the Bill of Rights provides for the protection of a set of liberties that were, at minimum, the primary motivation for the American Revolution. When the Declaration of Independence mentioned the "inalienable rights" that accrue to all human beings, it presaged the adoption of the first ten amendments to the Constitution. As a practical guide to the conduct of emergency powers, however, strict adherence to the Bill of Rights may be impossible and may constitute a threat to national security. In the past, administrations that exercised prerogative powers in times of emergency found themselves in the difficult position of either explaining why their violations of liberties were not beyond the scope of the Constitution or, lacking a plausible constitutional excuse, why their violations were temporary and absolutely necessary for national survival. In regard to suspension of individual liberties in times of emergency, there is a significant body of judicial precedent. Individuals often sought redress in the courts for damages visited upon them by the government in times of emergency. As I shall argue, the courts managed to reconcile the irreconcilable in most of these cases by taking a position that both hearkens back to the Constitution and allows for the exercise of extraordinary powers including the suspension of individual liberties.

Despite the fact that there exists a broad basis for establishing the existence of and defining prerogative powers in the modern

American context, there is a significant gap in the existing scholarship in this regard.[15] Americans tend to avoid this subject because the notion of prerogative powers exercised in reality challenges our notions and predilections toward government in the abstract. One obstacle to the discussion of prerogative powers in the United States is a failure to conceive of a separate set of discrete governmental responsibilities defined as prerogatives. The failure to recognize the existence of prerogative powers, however, does not eliminate the possibility that prerogative powers exist and must sometimes be exercised. Medieval and Enlightenment thinkers had a very clear idea of the meaning and, thus, the limits of prerogative powers. They believed that prerogative powers were to be exercised by the prince for the protection of the state and the good of its citizens. Furthermore, under the appropriate circumstances, these prerogatives could be exercised to the derogation of the rights of citizens.[16]

To admit to such a definition of prerogative in the American context would be to challenge some of our notions of constitutionalism. After all, to recognize the existence of situations beyond "unalterable law" would be to recognize a higher law beyond the Constitution. Such a notion is acceptable in Great Britain where the Constitution exists as a set of statutes, an amorphous set of historical precedents, and societal understandings. However, in the United States, to admit to existence of extraconstitutional powers would be to subvert the rule of law under the written constitution.

In American legal scholarship the predominant guideline for the settlement of claims is based on the principle that there are a set of neutral, nonpolitical conventions based in law through which the courts settle disputes.[17] Thus, the courts that adhere to these neutral principles in making their decisions avoid the appearance of infringing on the rights of the political branches of government. In the tradition of *stare decisis,* or the requirement that the court adhere to past decisions, case law becomes the empirical standard upon which the courts justify their decisions. Prerogative powers, however, exist by definition beyond precedent and outside the law. The courts, then, are placed in the un-comfortable position of reconciling their legal doctrines and case law to controversies for which there are no reliable precedents. The courts are forced, in ruling on the exercise of prerogative powers, to construct principles of law that both obfuscate the limits of prerogative powers—as any act can be justified given a creative-enough reading of the Constitution—and make a mockery of the rule of law.[18]

Walter Bagehot, in comparing the American and English constitutions, suggested that one of the great defects of the American Constitution is its inflexibility. This inflexibility does not render American government incapable of action in case of emergency. However, when extraordinary situations (not specifically prescribed by law) arise, the American government is forced "to frame absurd fictions to evade the plain sense of mischievous clauses [of the Constitution]."[19] By not admitting that there are circumstances outside the Constitution that require the government to act, we are forced to perform what are in essence illegal acts in order to save ourselves. This reality creates a conflict reflected in the American legal tradition. The courts, in their decisions, are forced to create "absurd fictions" to justify within the constitutional framework the exercise of what in most other countries would be considered legitimate exercises of prerogative powers.

Legal scholars in the United States are not well prepared to deal systematically with the consequences of the exercise of prerogative powers. Without any agreement that there *are* prerogative powers and limits to those powers, in emergencies the American government acts without legal guidance. If it is possible to argue that the exercise of prerogatives exists within a separate category of governmental powers, and if there exists some set of standards by which to guide the use of prerogative powers, a number of heretofore intractable constitutional questions may be answered. At the very least, a general guide to the use of prerogative powers may legitimate, in advance, the use of extraordinary powers in case of emergency.

A second reason that Americans, in particular, tend to eschew a comprehensive analysis of prerogative powers is that it offers an inherent challenge to the liberal philosophy and democratic doctrine upon which the structure of the state was built. For Americans, there is no satisfactory answer to the question, What are the limits to the exercise of emergency powers? The liberal doctrines upon which the United States was founded contain an internal dilemma. Even if we agree that a government which governs best, governs least, there are some times when governmental intervention is essential. Even strict libertarians recognize that self-protection provides at least one good reason for a state to form.[20] The problem for liberals in constructing a viable state is that the provision of security, domestic and external, requires vesting the state with the power to violate absolute property rights. After all, the state must be able to fund police forces and national armies through taxes. It is not clear, however, where the state's taxing power (or power to determine any outcomes that involve the distribution of goods) begins and where it ends. In fact, some of the greatest, unresolved debates in the liberal tradition revolve around this liberty-security nexus. The controversy over the limits of emergency powers is part of this debate to the extent that the exercise of powers in a threatening situation may involve the violation of liberties. For example, Abraham Lincoln imposed a variety of restrictions on individuals living in the Northeast in the immediate aftermath of the shelling of Fort Sumter. Such actions may have been necessary in the practical sense, but were they proper within the American constitutional scheme?

Prerogative powers are difficult to discuss, let alone define, in a society that cannot agree about how much liberty should be sacrificed for the sake of security. Our liberal tradition does not even provide us with the language required for this type of discussion. Representative of the liberal struggle with this dilemma of liberty versus security is John Stuart Mill's deliberation on the rights of the individual in his essay *On Liberty*. In his examination of the limits of the authority of society over the individual Mill argues: "Each [the individual and society] will receive its proper share, if each has that which more particularly concerns it. To individuality should belong the part of life in which it is chiefly the individual that is interested; to society, the part which chiefly interests society."[21] This construct is hardly adequate to delineate the boundary that exists between the public and private realm in a liberal society, but it does accurately illustrate the dilemma posed by the trade-off. Not even Mill was entirely faithful to this construct. Indeed, Mill came to the conclusion (as do most other liberals) that liberties cannot be unlimited and that a government might be permitted to, for example, restrict the freedom of expression in a society for the sake of public morals.

Central to the controversy in liberalism over the liberty-security nexus is the careful delineation of the public and private realms. Presumably, the government should have the authority to regulate matters that exist in the public's sphere of interest. However, the relationship between the public and private realm is difficult to define, in part, because the relationship between society and the individual is constantly changing. For example, international-relations theorists discuss the changing responsibilities of the state in the nuclear age. No longer is the state able to defend its borders against the onslaught of air power. As citizens become targets in the age of air attack, citizen populations, particularly in industrialized states, become strategic assets. In order to protect itself, the state must nurture and, at times, control its population for the sake of national security. This requirement will necessarily change the relationship between the citizen and the state and, thus, the boundaries between the public and private realm. Of course, the framers of the Constitution could not have foreseen the advent of air power.[22] The character of the threat to the nation and, consequently, the potential for the abuse of emergency powers has substantially evolved since the founding of the republic. Therefore, in the modern era, issues involving the exercises of prerogative power are both a reprise of a classic debate and a departure into a new realm because of the varying nature of the challenges to our liberal values and the democratic state.

The concept of boundaries of prerogative powers, therefore, is constantly changing in the liberal state. Matters that were once regarded to be entirely within the private realm, such as management and labor relations, are now considered to be properly within the purview of the government. Matters that were once considered to be intensely public, such as the race, gender, or religious affiliation of public officials (so much so that some people were, by law, excluded from public office), are now considered to be either irrelevant or to be treated as irrelevant for the distribution of public goods. This constant change in public philosophy renders the immutable edicts of our Constitution transmutable and again calls into question our concept of constitutionalism. The prerogative powers of government exist at the cutting edge of shifts in the boundaries of the public and private realms.

The framers were not so naive as to think that the Bill of Rights alone (should it be adopted) would be adequate to defend individual liberties. In fact, a motion to include a Bill of Rights in the Constitution was overwhelmingly rejected in the final days of the Constitutional Convention. What the framers built instead into the Constitution was a series of procedural safeguards designed to protect against the usurpation of power.[23] We are accustomed to thinking about these protections as the separation of powers and checks and balances systems. This emphasis on process very much reflected the mechanistic propensities of Enlightenment thinkers. To the extent that government was a machine for the provision of goods, it could be designed to prevent the type of malfunction that had led to the violation of individual rights (in this case, those rights of the American colonists) by that government which the framers considered most perfect (that of Great Britain). This faith in the shielding properties of process is a recurrent theme in American politics. The Constitution and any one of a number of state governments designed in the post-convention era reflected this reliance on countervailing structures as a protection against governmental excess.

When applied to the exercise of prerogative powers, however, this reliance on process and structure simply does not work. The exercise of emergency powers is not always conducive to a checks and balances design. Therefore, because Americans tend to equate proper procedure with democracy, there is, again, a certain degree of dissonance associated with the notion that the exercise of prerogative power may require the violation of due process. Americans are faced with the conclusion that sometimes our government is forced to perform what from the liberal perspective are undemocratic acts.

Of course, democratic theory is quite flexible. For example, it would be hard to argue that Britain, even in the absence of a separation of powers and a written constitution, is not a democracy. The prerogative powers exercised by the prime minister and her cabinet are, for the most part, constitutional. One solution, therefore, to the dilemma of the exercise of prerogative power in the United States would be to replace the presidential structure of government with a parliamentary design. However, suggestions to this effect are anathema in the United States.[24] At the very least, the potential unintended consequences of such a fundamental reform should dictate a high degree of caution.

It is more likely in making this comparison to come to the conclusion that both the United States and Britain, despite the dissimilarities in their political systems, share an important attribute. While our two constitutions are different, the notion of constitutionalism as it applies to both states is very much the same. Constitutional democracies have the ability to withstand extraordinary threats because constitutionalism has both its legal and contractual components. By "contractual component" I refer to the shared values and notions of justice common to a society that form the basis for a social contract and the legitimacy of government. In the United States, we tend to focus on the legal, structural components of our Constitution to the exclusion of the contractual component. Woodrow Wilson once described the American attitudes toward the Constitution as "an undiscriminating and almost blind worship of its principles."[25] Indeed, because we tend, in some sense, to worship the document itself, we tend to overlook the very important contractual components of our Constitution that come into play when our formal structures of government are bypassed.

As an alternative to a blind worship of constitutional text, a frank discussion of the nature and limits of prerogative powers serves our political system in several ways. Because the courts are often reluctant to intervene in disputes between the executive and legislative branches, these "political questions" are supposed to be settled through conflict and cooperation between the coordinate political branches. All too often the result of this competition is either gridlock or illegality. For noncrisis decision making, a government frozen in dispute is at least not a direct threat to national security. However, when issues of national survival are involved, gridlock becomes a threat thereto and illegal acts performed by our government to circumvent deadlock become a threat to our liberties. Given the volatility of the international environment and our recent experiences with the conduct of covert and possibly illegal activities in the White House, it seems possible that our political system alone is incapable of providing a limit to the exercise of prerogative powers. Therefore, a systematic outline of prerogative powers can serve as a guide for government officials. If prerogative powers are more clearly understood, representatives can anticipate the response to, and plan for the use of, emergency powers. Nothing will prevent for all situations the tendency of some governmental officials to commit illegal acts. Nor will it be possible to plan in advance for all emergencies. However, a thorough discussion of the limits and exercise of prerogative powers will help prevent the abuse of powers that arises from honest misunderstandings.

2 From King to Country: The Transfer of Plenary Powers

I have already suggested that between the Middle Ages and the founding of the United States, the idea of the proper exercise of prerogative powers underwent a fundamental change. My suggestion, however, does not capture the richness and complexity of that transition. To provide for the exercise of emergency powers in a democracy requires the construction of an institutional design of extraordinary subtlety and balance. The American Constitution, as it was originally written, reflects an attempt on the part of its framers to create this sort of equilibrium.

In order to guarantee the protection of liberties and at the same time provide the state with the wherewithal to protect itself, the framers had to accommodate several concerns. First and foremost, they were cognizant of the need for extraordinary authorities in government. They were not so naive as to think that democratic process alone could protect the state in case of emergency. Second, they were very much aware of the potential for the abuse of executive powers. Consequently, they were intent on designing a system for the exercise of governmental powers, including extraordinary powers, in which the authorities of government were shared. Third, they were charged with the politically sensitive task of reconciling a revolutionary regime to the demands of practical governing. In order to construct a politically viable and, at the same time, workable constitution, the framers had to design a government that would at least appear to preserve the principles of the Revolution. This last task was, perhaps, the most difficult. One of the greatest successes of the Constitutional Convention was that these demands on constitutional construction were more or less satisfied. The key to the framers' success in this regard, I shall argue, was their ability to adapt an essential component of democratic rule, the social contract, to the political and practical vagaries of eighteenth-century America.

The American Constitution was not constructed from whole cloth. The framers were accomplished students of history and of philosophy as well as being experienced politicians. Their work in designing the Constitution was heavily imbued with the intellectual ferment sweeping Europe at the time. The renowned works of Hume, Locke, Burke, Montesquieu, Coke, and others were widely circulated and discussed in the colonies. In fact, many of the obstacles the framers confronted in designing our system of government were at the same time the focus of heated debates among philosophers contemporary to the American Revolution. In designing the Constitution, the framers selected ideas from many of the contributors to this debate. They also added, for good measure, a dose of their own strategy seasoned by their experience with the Articles of Confederation, colonial, and state governments. Nonetheless, it would be fair to say the framers did not design the Constitution as a separate political or philosophical tradition so much as they made innovative use of existing doctrines.[1] Consequently, the American Constitution is really one step along a beaten path. As such, in trying to determine the founders' intent, we must examine the context in which their decisions were made.

To understand the structure of the executive branch in the American Constitution (or the other institutional designs of government, for that matter), we must understand the broad variety of philosophies and historical experiences that competed for expression. The founders were at the same time democrats and republicans, Whigs and radicals, liberals and conservatives, revolutionaries and aristocrats, and so on. Each of these perspectives had an influence on the final outcome. Above all, however, the framers were practical politicians. They had been active in state and colonial governments. Therefore, their solutions to problems of constitutional design were practical and contained not a little compromise. In the case of prerogative powers the framers designed an eminently practical solution: without admitting that prerogative powers existed (these authorities were associated in the American mind with the colonial rule of the British king), they created within the constitutional system a government fully empowered to exercise a set of functional prerogatives that could be brought to bear in response to the unforeseen.

For subjects of a monarch in the Middle Ages the limits and responsibilities for the exercise of prerogative powers were clearly established. According to one medieval jurist, the king had the absolute power to make laws, to make peace and war, to create supreme magistrates, to be the court of last appeal, to pardon offenses, to coin money, to have allegiance, fealty, and homage, and to impose taxes.[2] Prerogative powers permitted the king to exceed the established laws of the state. This was considered permissible inasmuch as the king, as the embodiment of the state, was a representative of God on Earth.[3] When situations arose that demanded plenary action, no one questioned the right of the king to act or the duty of subjects to obey. Subjects were protected from arbitrary, tyrannical rule by the Deity. Despotic rule was equated with natural calamity such as flood or pestilence.

By the beginning of the seventeenth century in England the notion of the divine right of kings had begun to erode. Already prior to the Glorious Revolution there existed an influential school of thought that the king's power was limited by a separate law of God or natural law.[4] Under duress, the prerogative of the king in England had been subordinated to the baronetcy, a system formalized in 1215 under the Magna Carta. In addition, the power of the central government was limited in the Middle Ages simply because of the absence of mechanisms for state control. Often, criminal justice, property rights, and levies were administered locally because reach of the king was physically limited.

In addition, scientific discoveries associated with the Enlightenment and the Protestant Reformation brought about a challenge to the traditional notions of authority. No longer was it

completely clear that man was an unwitting pawn of divine powers. Advances in science enabled individuals to understand and
even change the world around them. This notion of empowerment sealed the fate of the already weakened absolute monarch.
If man through science could control nature, humans through
self-government could control their own nation's fate. No longer
was it necessary for subjects to suffer the caprice of incompetent
or misguided rulers. Of course, the effects of this feeling of empowerment were slow to become manifest. The earliest indicators
of this Enlightenment influence came in the psychic separation of
the king from heaven. No longer was it necessarily true that the
king acted as a spokesman for God. For example, Francis Bacon
writing in the early seventeenth century suggested:

Princes are like heavenly bodies, which cause good and evil times; and
which have much veneration, but no rest. All precepts concerning kings
are in effect comprehended in those two remembrances, remember that
thou art a man and remember that thou art a god or a representative of
God; the one bridleth their power and the other their will.[5]

The very recognition that kings were mortals, driven by mortal
passions and subject to some sort of outside, temporal control
endangered the institution of the monarchy. Even though Bacon's
statement is by no means a blanket indictment of the monarchy
(Bacon was lord chancellor under James I), it is not difficult to
envision a number of policy or structural consequences of the notion that the king's powers, including the prerogative power,
were not exercised by divine right and could be controlled.

One such consequence of this changing conception of the
king's role was the evolution of the belief that the king's power
could be modified and limited. For example, it was argued particularly by parliamentarians in England that a distinction could
be made between the "absolute" and "ordinary" prerogatives of
the king. The absolute prerogative was to be the king's authority
to act outside the common law for reasons of state. "Reasons of
state" in this case included not only emergencies, but other areas
of public policy traditionally associated with the king's authority
as well. For example, the administration of crown property was

considered to be subsumed under the king's absolute prerogative.[6] The ordinary prerogative was to include those actions taken
by the king pursuant to existing law and subject to review by
magistrates or Parliament. In essence, because the exercise of the
ordinary prerogative was subject to review, the king was to be
stripped of his power to govern the daily lives of subjects. His
prerogative powers were to be reserved for emergencies, cere-
monial occasions, and the administration of kingly estates.

This distinction between the absolute and ordinary prerogatives, however, was not universally accepted. Royalists refused to
recognize any formalized limits to the king's prerogative, while
radicals refused to recognize any aspect of the king's prerogative
as being unlimited.[7] More often than not, because the king did
not recognize any limits to his prerogative, he simply ignored any
limits thought to exist by Parliament. Eventually, the dissension
over the king's flouting of law exploded into the Puritan Revolution, which rocked England in the 1640s, culminating in the
Glorious Revolution and the overthrow of the Stuarts in 1688.
While most parliamentarians agreed that there were some occasions that required the exercise of prerogative powers by the king,
many of the exercises of prerogative powers by the king in the
early seventeenth century challenged even the broadest notions of
the king's prerogative. Of particular concern was the king's tendency to prorogue Parliament at just the moment a bill unfavor-
able to the king's interests was to be voted.[8] One particularly
egregious example in this regard involved Parliament's attempt to
regulate the levies set on foreign commerce.

Tariffs were traditionally collected for and by the king, pursuant to the royal prerogative. Fearing that the king's levies on
the increasingly high levels of foreign trade would free the king
of his dependence on parliamentary taxation, an attempt was
made in 1610 to vote a bill that would require the king to clear
with Parliament all levies on trade. King James I simply dissolved
Parliament before the vote could be taken.[9] Ultimately, in 1629,
Parliament passed three resolutions intended to deny the force of
the king's levy of "tunnage and poundage" (as the king's tariffs

were known). However, in order to pass those resolutions, the Speaker, who served as an agent of the king in Parliament, had to be physically restrained. The leaders of the parliamentary majority responsible for these actions were arrested and imprisoned. Parliament was dissolved and what ensued were the eleven years of the "personal government" of Charles I.

For the most part, the notion of an absolute royal prerogative died in England with Charles I in 1649. The mere fact that the king's person was not inviolate destroyed a psychic barrier that had heretofore existed. From that point onward, royalists were forced to fight a rear-guard action in making the increasingly awkward argument that the king's power was absolute, divinely inspired. For example, Sir Robert Filmer defended the powers of the king by arguing that the relationship between the king and his subjects was essentially paternal. Subjects could no more choose their king than they could choose their parents. Upon achieving their majority, subjects transferred their obedience from father to king. According to Filmer, the only temporal recourse for subjects harmed by the king's authority was the confidence that the offending monarch would be divinely punished.[10]

On the other hand, the challenges to royalist authority were not so clear-cut. After all, to design a government bereft of kingly rule was to chart a new course. Some revolutionaries in Parliament called for a "mixed" government in which ruling powers were to be shared with or wielded exclusively by the House of Commons. This demand for the rule of the Commons could be easily misinterpreted in the modern context. Membership in the House of Commons was restricted to landed subjects below the rank of peer who had incomes in excess of forty shillings a year. These property requirements probably excluded 80 to 90 percent of the rural population.[11] Consequently, the call for a "mixed government," in which powers were to be shared among the estates in government, was by no means a call for democracy as we know it. The majority of parliamentary revolutionaries were not "levellers" and had no desire to share power with the masses. Indeed, objections to the inequality of suffrage in Great Britain were not really resolved until the last half of the nineteenth century.[12]

Others in the revolutionary ranks appealed to a fundamental law that transcended Parliament or the monarchy. For them, Parliament was merely a cipher or a court of last resort for the interpretation of fundamental law. Furthermore, those parliamentarians who believed in the precedence of natural law argued that a contract in society existed such that government (and the king in particular) was bound to abide by the higher law or be overthrown. For example, Sir Edward Coke, chief justice until 1616 and later a member of Parliament, argued that because common law existed above parliamentary law, the courts could find acts of Parliament against common law and, therefore, void. As we shall see, Coke's judicial opinion in the Bonham case was well known in America at the time of the American Revolution; even though his theories were discarded in England (the proponents of the sovereignty of Parliament came to dominate), his arguments would be used to defend the principle of judicial review in the United States nearly two hundred years later.[13]

It is at the time of the Glorious Revolution that the British and subsequent theories of American government began to diverge. The fact that the structure of American government under the Constitution bears a superficial resemblance to the mixed government that emerged in the aftermath of the Glorious Revolution is misleading. In fact, American colonials were more likely to be followers of Coke than of Sir John Eliot and the other parliamentarians.[14] Without parliamentary representation, and buffeted by the king's ministers' exercises of the royal prerogative, the colonials had little choice but to appeal to a higher moral or common law. Presumably, if there existed "higher" law governing the behavior of states, the royal prerogative was limited. Thus, through a belief in the supremacy of law, colonials had a foundation upon which to base their complaints against—and eventually their resistance to—the rule of the British king.

At the time of the American Revolution, British and colonial political philosophy began to divide on yet another issue. The parliamentarian supporters of mixed government and the royalists in Britain actually had much in common: in particular, both argued explicitly that no "contract" existed between a ruler and the ruled. There were several reasons that the notion of a social contract was dangerous to a monarch or an oligarchy (such as it existed under the rule of Parliament). For one thing, such a contract would imply a mutual obligation such that a government could be held to a certain standard of behavior with regard to its subjects. To imply that such a standard existed, would be to challenge the absolute sovereignty of Parliament or the king.

A presumption that the relationship between the king and subject was contractual was also dangerous for royalists and the oligarchy. Such a premise presupposed some kind of voluntary relationship. If a societal contract existed, it would follow that a relationship voluntarily entered into could be voluntarily broken. In addition, the parties to a contract cannot be said to enter into that agreement freely unless there accrues from that understanding some kind of mutual advantage. The mutual advantage of a contract is undermined if one side of the contract (the king's obligations) is open-ended. Therefore, contract theory makes absolute monarchy or the absolute sovereignty of Parliament impossible. Presumably, if one could accept the idea of a contractual relationship between the ruler and the ruled, one could accept the possibility that the exercise of the king's prerogative powers could be challenged as a violation of the social contract.[15]

The establishment of a social contract, then, is essential for the establishment of a constitutional democracy. In order for a people to govern itself there must be a certain underlying consensus that contributes to stability. Citizens must agree to disagree or at least find some way to accept peaceably the inevitable compromises that come of democratic decision making. If the disadvantages of social-contract theory were obvious to monarchs, the advantages of the contract for liberals and democratic theorists were just as apparent. Simply put, the social contract guaranteed the loyalty and cooperation of citizens without requiring coercion or an increasingly preposterous mythology of divine right.

There were attempts to reconcile these advantages of the social contract with notions of absolute rule. For example, Thomas Hobbes, who was no great champion of democratic theory, attempted to incorporate contract theory into his plan for a commonwealth. However, his social contract was intended to be without the "warts" that would undermine absolute authority. As a result, his plan for commonwealth as outlined in the *Leviathan* contains what are, from the modern democratic perspective, some very unsatisfactory compromises. According to Hobbes, a commonwealth was formed when every person made the following commitment to every other person: "I authorise and give up my Right of Governing my selfe, to this Man, or to this Assembly of men, on this condition, that thou give up thy Right to him, and Authorise all his Actions in like manner."[16] This was not a fully encompassing social contract at all because it failed to constrain the ruler(s) of society. Only citizens made a commitment to one another in a kind of social compact. Furthermore, according to Hobbes, such a contract once entered into remained in force (including being passed on from one generation to another) until such time as the sovereign was unable to protect his subjects. The only implicit agreement that existed between the rulers and the ruled in Hobbes's *Leviathan* was a guarantee of protection in exchange for sovereignty.

Hobbes's vision rested on the notion that the state had to possess absolute and irrevocable power. Consequently, the Hobbesian compact represented very little practical departure from the philosophy of divine right. When rulers enjoyed absolute sovereignty, the potential for the abuse of power was enormous. Only if the compact included the rulers as well as the ruled could a government exist for the protection of personal freedoms and for the protection of property. This is precisely the point made by John Locke in his *Second Treatise of Government*.

For Locke the state of nature could exist in either peace or war. If men lived according to reason and to equity, the state of nature would remain at peace. However, if individuals violated these *natural laws*, disorder would result. In the state of nature, each individual was responsible for enforcing these natural laws. However, it might be more convenient for individuals to form freely associated commonwealths or compacts in which citizens agreed among themselves to delegate to a legislature and magistrates the power to interpret and execute the law. In a departure from Hobbes and others who believed that the absolute authority of a prince was the only way to protect and stabilize society, Locke had subtly changed the nature of the social contract. No longer was the social contract to be entered into between the ruler and the ruled or between the subjects of the state to the exclusion of the ruling class. Rather, the social contract in Locke's society was to be made between the citizens of the state, none of whom enjoyed a special status by virtue of their position in government. The government, therefore, was to be part of rather than separate from or above civil society.

An absolute monarch could not exist in such a community. In fact, according to Locke, unrestrained monarchs existed in a warring state of nature because "there is no judge to be found, no appeal lies open to any one, who may fairly, and indifferently, and with authority decide" the fate of the prince.[17] He believed that such unrestrained power would inevitably be abused. The fact that the absolute monarch interacted in an unequal relationship with the rest of the community meant that society was "exposed to all the misery and inconveniences, that a man can fear from one, who being in the unrestrained state of nature, is yet corrupted with flattery, and armed with power."[18] Such a corrupted authority was to be properly resisted by force. Thus, the prince with unrestricted power would ultimately bring about a domestic state of war or rebellion.

Locke had broken a barrier. By arguing that people associated with one another by virtue of a social contract he was arguing, in effect, that despotic rule could be challenged and that all individuals were equal (in terms of rights if not in possessions). By defining and defending the notion of natural rights he held the government of contractual commonwealths responsible to a certain standard of conduct.[19] Because civil government served at the pleasure of citizens, a corrupt government could and should be overthrown. Locke best summed up the standard to which government was to be held when he wrote: "The state of nature has a law to govern it, which obliges every one: and reason, which is that law, teaches all mankind, who will but consult it, that being all equal and independent, no one ought to harm another in his life, health, liberty, or possessions."[20] While Locke's *Second Treatise* was important to the Whig Revolution in 1688, his writings were just as important to the American Revolution. More than eighty years after their publication, Locke's writings (and those of other liberal authors of his day) were turned against the English themselves to become one of the primary philosophical justifications for the overthrow of the English monarchy in America. Contract theory was the seedbed of the American Revolution. The king, by virtue of his violation of fundamental rights, had abdicated his license to rule in the colonies.

There were, nonetheless, a number of practical problems associated with actually implementing Locke's design for government. In particular, it was not entirely clear how government was to respond to emergencies and how the use of emergency powers was to be controlled. Locke came to the conclusion that the legislative branch should be the ultimate source of all authority in government. However, when faced with a threat that challenged the survival of the state the executive branch of government might be allowed to respond without the express permission of the legislature. Furthermore, it might be necessary for rulers "to do several things, of their own free choice where the law was silent, and sometimes too against the direct letter of the law, for the public good. . . . a good prince, who is mindful of the trust put into his hands, and careful of the good of his people, cannot have too much prerogative, that is, power to do good."[21] But if a ruler promoted through the use of prerogative "an interest distinct from that of the public," the public could reclaim its rights. However, as long as the prerogative of the state was properly exercised, its existence would be "tacitly" tolerated.[22]

Locke's dilemma in regards to prerogative powers was that natural law imposes a restraint on government that may not be realistic. State survival may create the need for short-term sacrifice for the sake of long-term good. Locke was simply willing to cede to the executive in government the power to perform illegal acts in case of emergency. That design, to be sure, contained some important internal contradictions. First, to allow the executive to violate the law in the exercise of prerogative powers would be to admit that, in fact, natural law was not the limit of governmental action. Yet Locke was very clear in his emphasis on the supremacy of natural rights. Furthermore, to allow the executive to wield prerogative powers would be to challenge the sovereignty of the legislative branch.

On the eve of the American Revolution, rebellious patriots were in no position to ponder the intricacies of building a governing regime that was internally consistent. The justification for revolt provided in the *Second Treatise* was enough. As we shall see, building structures for the governing of the state was a secondary concern at the start of the Revolution. Only after the end of the fighting did the problem of erecting a proper system of governing become preeminent.

The Declaration of Independence reflected the uncertainty surrounding the establishment of a new, American sovereignty. To the extent that the Declaration recognized the rights of individuals to "life, liberty, and the pursuit of happiness," it embraced the concept of natural rights, but only in a very general, ephemeral sense. That the Declaration failed to mention the right to property was a direct departure from the purest form of Lockean liberalism. Most of the Declaration was a count-by-count indictment of abuses specific to the rule of George III rather than a statement of governing principles. No explicit mention was made of the corrupting influence of the monarchic system in general nor of the misuses of power by Parliament. Instead, the Declaration sought to disassociate the colonies from a specific tyrannical ruler and, thus, separate America from the British Empire. The Declaration, therefore, was very limited, containing neither a full statement of natural rights nor a commitment to the establishment of any particular type of governing system.

Thomas Jefferson was clearly sidestepping a commitment to any prearranged form of government in writing the Declaration. Instead, he left the door open for a practical government, one based on popular consent but not necessarily beyond executive control or representative institutions. In a letter to Henry Lee, Jefferson summed up his intentions in composing the Declaration:

This was the object of the Declaration of Independence. Not to find out new principles, or new arguments, never before thought of, not merely to say things which had never been said before; but to place before mankind the common sense of the subject, in terms so plain and firm as to command their assent, and to justify ourselves in the independent stand we are compelled to take. . . . it was intended to be an expression of the American mind.[23]

The Declaration *was* very much a reflection of the American mind. Americans were not radicals. In fact, it is sometimes said that the American Revolution was a conservative revolution.[24] For former Englishmen, the rejection of the monarchy or an active executive proved much too drastic. The theories of Locke were useful insofar as they were used to justify the revolution. But a government bound by natural law might become frozen in inaction or in danger of overthrow.

From the perspective of more temperate revolutionaries it was commonly thought that the problems the colonies were having with Britain were not so much the fault of the monarch as they were the consequence of the abuse of power by the king's advisers. Specifically, ministers of the crown had usurped the prerogatives of the crown and, thereby, undermined the independence of the House of Commons.[25] From the colonials' perspective, the problem with the British handling of the colonies was really a technical one. Because the administration of the crown's colonies traditionally fell within the purview of the king's prerogative, British subjects living in the colonies were subject to the king's (primarily the king's ministers') will without parliamentary re-course.[26] The power of the crown had been abused to be sure, but there was still very little sympathy for the idea that the executive, or even extraordinary powers, should be done away with. Instead, proper representation would alleviate the more egregious exercise of prerogative power by the king.

The emphasis, therefore, in forming postrevolutionary state governments was on placing controls on rather than doing away with the executive. Most of the power of government at the state level was to be concentrated in the legislative branch. Very few state constitutions allowed for a powerful, independent chief executive (with the notable exception of New York). Gubernatorial power was to be severely restricted but not to the extent that Paine or Rousseau had contemplated.[27] Only at the national level, in the Articles of Confederation, were there no provisions for an executive branch at all.

It would be easy to misinterpret the absence of executive institutions in the Articles of Confederation as a dismissal of executive power. However, for what they were intended, the Articles were well suited. They were designed in haste (first proposed in 1777 and finally ratified by every state in 1781) to facilitate the conduct of the Revolution. As such, the Articles were intended to coordinate the management of foreign affairs among the colonies.[28] However, much of the conduct of the Revolution was functionally out of the hands of the Continental Congress. The greatest portion of the responsibility for foreign and military affairs during the Revolution was left to the military under the command of General Washington, the various state militias under local command, and to a few luminaries of the Revolution who were sent as emissaries to select European capitals. The conduct of domestic and internal affairs at the start of the Revolution were really secondary concerns. Even under colonial rule most domestic policy initiatives remained in the hands of local governments. The Articles, therefore, represented a temporary compromise that filled a void, a relatively minor coordinating role, created by the forced departure of the king's ministers. It would be inaccurate, therefore, to suggest that the Articles were the "first" American Constitution.

The success of the Revolution created needs for governing beyond the state constitutions and the Articles of Confederation. In particular, there was an evident need for the creation of some sort of coordinating or executive function at the national level. There were two general problems with the postrevolutionary emphasis on the legislative function. Legislative institutions were structurally deficient in the execution of the laws; more important, legislatures were just as likely to abuse their privilege as were corrupted monarchs.[29] Consequently, when the time came for building a more permanent, viable structure for governing, the framers of the Constitution and, indeed, much of the citizenry, were more amenable to the incorporation of executive power. The Articles, which had been adequate for managing a collection of largely independent states, were inadequate for governing a more economically integrated United States. In the absence of a colonial master, the country required a structure of more centralized control.

In designing the new national government, the Constitutional Convention looked to the precedents established in the states. On the basis of that experience it was obvious that there was clearly a role at the national level for an executive who, at times, could exercise plenary powers. The problem remaining for the framers was the old liberal dilemma of balancing the power of government and the liberties of the citizenry. In crafting a Constitution that provided for an executive authority and centralized power, the framers were obligated to proceed with caution.

The revolutionaries of France and the United States were particularly sensitive to the abuses of power by the executive in government. While they were anxious to promote the notion of natural rights as a justification for revolt against the king, they were very reluctant to restore, in the aftermath of their revolutions, the powers of the executive branch. For example, within Jean Jacques Rousseau's *Of the Social Contract,* the "prince" was not sovereign and served only at the pleasure of the assembly.[30]

Because the prince was no more than a delegate, he was not to be an executive in the tradition of a prime minister or a king. Rousseau's "legislator," a sort of psychic guide to the nation, was to inspire the General Assembly within the "general will." The legislator was also not to be an executive in the traditional sense; instead, the assembly was to perform the executive function and guide the "prince" in carrying out its will.

While an emphasis on natural rights contributed an important justification for revolt, such an emphasis did not necessarily serve the purposes of the state. Rousseau attempted to deal with the inconsistency of, on the one hand, promoting natural rights and, on the other, empowering the nation to act in case of emergency. For him, the decisions of the assembly guided by the "general will" were sufficient for the protection of the rights of citizens. In Rousseau's society reliance on the performance of the assembly constituted a kind of floating social contract. The assembly set the limits of the social contract that could be adjusted according to the environmental context. This "contractual flexibility" provided a procedural and philosophical justification for the exercise of prerogative power in a democracy. As long as the assembly approved an action, that action existed within the general will. Rousseau's social contract was, therefore, a procedural contract. Rousseau thus made an occasional illegal exercise of power (in Locke's opinion) completely legal.

Thomas Paine was to limit the executive function differently. Paine incited a nation to revolt by arguing that, as a system of government, "monarchy and succession have laid but the world in blood and ashes."[31] He believed that any system of monarchy, including Britain's mixed government, was illegitimate. Government was to be run by a legislative assembly. The only responsibility of the president would be that of presiding officer over the legislature. Unlike Rousseau, Paine did not dismiss the notion of representative rule; he had to provide a model of a government for a continent-sized state. Faced with the practical problems of governing the former colonies, Paine had no choice but to risk the problems associated with representative rule.[32]

"Every age and every generation must be free to act for itself," wrote Paine in *The Rights of Man*. Both Rousseau and Paine believed that the responsibility of government was to accommodate every generation in pursuit of its own special political and social needs. The actions of a government were only to be carried out at the behest of the citizenry at a particular point in time. Governments under a flexible contract could take any actions necessary in pursuit of national survival.[33] A constitution had to be flexible enough to provide for emergencies and contextual changes in a way that a contract based on natural rights could not. Indeed, Paine was clearly disappointed that, after the Revolution, the Constitution had become "a political bible" and that Americans had become literal in their dedication to it.

Thus, in comparing the societal constructs of Rousseau and Paine on the one hand and Locke on the other, we see that all three theorists in one way or another were willing to place almost unlimited powers in the hands of the state. It was not clear, however, to what extent the natural rights of citizens could be violated for the good of the state. Neither was it clear what sort of procedural safeguards should be established for the protection of liberties: Locke had simply conceded to government the latitude to commit illegal acts; Rousseau and Paine had basically provided for a procedural contract, the limits of which were not clearly established. Because neither of these arrangements imposed limits on the exercise of extraordinary powers, neither was acceptable to the framers.

For the solution to this problem, the framers turned to a mechanical-structural device. Government could be designed according to engineering principles such that power could be balanced against power and ambition pitted against ambition. Like the panels of a roof, the branches of government could be made to lean against one another to create a stronger structure. The great contemporary proponent of this structure was the oft-cited (particularly by the framers) Charles de Secondat, the baron de Montesquieu. Montesquieu presented all the advantages of Locke, Paine, and Rousseau and none of the problems. A government

structured according to Montesquieu's scheme was fully empowered and structurally designed for the protection of liberties. In
Spirit of the Laws Montesquieu argued that liberty could be built
into a government through the creation of a particular constitutional structure:

Neither democracy nor aristocracy is free by nature. Political liberty exists only in those governments where power is moderated. Even in them,
liberty is not always found. Political liberty exists only when there is no
abuse of power. . . . To prevent the abuse of power, things must be so
ordered that power checks power.[34]

The appeal of Montesquieu's construct over those of Locke and
Paine was that the separation of powers guarded against the dan-
gers of faction and, the same time, empowered government in no
other, comparable way.[35] Unlike Rousseau and Paine, Montesquieu rejected exclusive reliance on the legislative function. In addition, Montesquieu was very careful to avoid all reference to
natural rights as the basis of a social contract.[36] Unlike Locke,
Montesquieu's fundamental conviction was that structure in government would be the ultimate guard against the violation of liberties.

It is probable that the founders would have adopted some form
of separated powers had they never heard of Montesquieu.[37]
George Washington, as commander of the army, recognized in
the early days of the Revolution the structural deficiencies of a
national government without centralized control. In 1780, Washington wrote in a letter to James Duane, "there are two things (as
I have often declared) which in my opinion, are indispensably
necessary to the well being and good Government of our public
Affairs; these are, greater powers to Congress, and more responsibility and permanency in the executive bodies."[38] By 1781 Congress voted to establish ministerial posts with executive authority
over the conduct of war, foreign affairs, and finance. Because
Congress and the states refused to vest proper authority in these
departments, ministers appointed to these positions were difficult
to appoint and quick to resign. Robert Livingston resigned as secretary of foreign affairs in 1782. Robert Morris resigned as su-

perintendent of finance in 1783 and the secretary of the marine was permanently vacant. As it became clear that the Articles of Confederation were in need of reform, specifically in the direction of the establishment of an executive institution, proposals for the separation of powers structure as we now know it, began to emerge.

For one thing, the executive function under the new constitution was to be separated from the legislative branch. Too often during the Revolution, executive decision making had been beset by legislative disorder. This does not mean, however, that just because the executive was to be distinct from the legislative department that the powers of government were to be separated as well. Not only is it impossible to divine a clear division between legislative, executive, and judicial power, but it is also, according to the framers, inadvisable. In defending the separation of powers structure (in regards to the Senate's role in the trying of impeachments) in *Federalist* paper 66, Hamilton wrote, "this partial intermixture [of functions] is even, in some cases, not only proper but necessary to the mutual defense of the several members of the government against each other."[39]

Furthermore, the framers, and particularly Hamilton, did not establish even a clear conceptual distinction between the executive and legislative function. One of the main problems with Congress's monopoly of power under the Articles of Confederation was the tendency of the legislature to become occupied with the minutiae of legislation. In 1780 Hamilton, in criticizing the function of Congress under the Articles of Confederation, commented, "Congress have kept the power too much into their own hands and have meddled too much with details of every sort. Congress is properly a deliberative corps and it forgets itself when it attempts to play the executive."[40] The implication here is that the executive function, in fact, is little more than an extension of the legislative responsibility. Later on, in defending the new constitution, Hamilton did establish a separate role in the executive department distinct from that of the legislative branch. In *Federalist* paper 70, in defending the vigorous executive, he made reference to the essential role of the "dictator" in the Roman Republic.[41] That separate role, however, was a function of circumstance, not of a character distinct in the institution of the presidency. In *Federalist* paper 72, Hamilton wrote:

> The administration of government in its largest sense, comprehends all the operations of the body politic, whether legislative, executive, or judiciary; but in its most usual and perhaps in its most precise significa- tion it is limited to executive details, and fall peculiarly within the province of the executive department.[42]

The executive function was only a subset of the larger governmental function. As such, the powers of the executive were to be shared in the fullest sense. Even in the exercise of extraordinary powers, where the executive was likely to be at an advantage, there was no indication that Congress and the rest of the political structure should not participate. Even prerogative powers were to be shared.[43]

The question remained as to whether the separation of powers, as a process, was adequate to the task of the protecting, at the same time, the security of the state and the liberty of its citizens. This controversy was of particular importance in the debate at the end of the Constitutional Convention concerning a proposal to include in the final document a bill of rights. The decision by the convention *not* to include a bill of rights was, in the context of the founding, a remarkable and indicative decision.

As a product of the Enlightenment, the Constitution is singular in its omissions. In an era in which philosophers and even American patriots were obsessed with the concept of natural rights, the original Constitution omitted a bill of rights. There were, of course, disagreements at the time of the convention over this exclusion. Thomas Jefferson, who was not at the convention, and George Mason (who was the author of the Virginia Declaration of Rights) who was present, both disapproved of a constitution that did not include a bill of rights.[44] In the end, Mason refused to sign the Constitution and Jefferson complained vigorously about this omission in his letters to Madison. Madison, for his part, was relatively unenthusiastic about the inclusion of a declaration of rights in the Constitution. He simply did not think a bill of rights would serve any material purpose. In a letter to Jefferson he defended his position in this regard:

Supposing a bill of rights to be proper . . . I am inclined to think that *absolute* restrictions in cases that are doubtful, or where emergencies may overrule them, ought to be avoided. The restrictions however strongly marked on paper will never be regarded when opposed to the decided sense of the public, and after repeated violations in extraordinary cases they will lose even their ordinary efficacy. Should a Rebellion or insurrection alarm the people as well as the Government, and a suspension of the Habeas Corpus be dictated by the alarm, no written prohibitions on earth would prevent the measure. . . . The best security against these evils is to remove the pretext for them.[45]

For Madison a bill of rights would become a "parchment barrier" that would be debased by its inclusion in the Constitution.[46] While the Bill of Rights was eventually adopted as a political compromise necessary for the ratification of the Constitution, it is not inaccurate to suggest that the Bill of Rights was a secondary concern. The limit, then, in the exercise of prerogative powers was meant to exist in the process and structure of government.

The exercise of prerogative powers under the Constitution is the product of a cacophony of influence. The Glorious Revolution, in effect, transferred the prerogative powers of the king to the state. Because there was considerable disagreement over the rights to the exercise of those powers, and because American revolutionaries tended to subscribe to the philosophies of the minority factions in this debate, American politics diverges from the British model at this point. In Britain, the prerogative powers were transferred to the landed gentry as represented in the House of Commons. In America, the issue of the exercise of prerogative powers underwent an evolution between the time of the Revolution and the Constitutional Convention.[47] During the American Revolution, the rebels accepted the Lockean notion that George III's violation of colonists' natural rights was an abdication of his responsibilities. A belief in natural right was an important justification for revolt.

The Lockean construct, however, presented problems for the construction of a practical government. Because government, according to Locke, was constrained by natural law, extraordinary powers when exercised were, by definition, illegal and possibly a justification for revolt. Armed with the experience of government under the Articles of Confederation and state governments dominated by legislatures, the framers were convinced that there was a need for a central government empowered with the authority to act and, on occasion, go beyond natural law. For the framers, the model of government espoused by Montesquieu best fit their needs. The separation of powers was a structural safeguard against the dominance of faction. The emphasis on structure and process in government rather than on absolute rights made it possible for government to exercise extraordinary powers within the law.

The Constitution that emerged was largely a synthesis of Montesquieu's design and Locke's philosophy (to the extent that the two could be reconciled). The legislative powers that emerged from these machinations were clearly enumerated and extraordinarily wide-ranging. There was a certain consensus associated with the importance of the legislative function. No such consensus existed in regards to the executive power. The executive power was not well defined. This lack of focus with respect to the powers of the presidency almost certainly reflected the failure to settle a number of ongoing controversies. Besides, the framers knew that they could not plan in advance for all contingencies. Instead, they left for future generations the task of establishing the limits of the executive power. Fortunately, they did provide for an independent judiciary (one of the great innovations in the Constitution) that would become the arena in which much of this uncertainty was played out.

In the discussion that is to follow of the constitutionality of prerogative powers we must be willing to look beyond the confines of our sometimes limited written Constitution. Beneath the surface of the design of the presidency, the Congress, the judiciary, and the Bill of Rights lies a history of struggle and a very definite understanding of the need for the exercise of extraordinary powers. In other words, beneath the surface of the Constitution exists a contractual component that reconciles Locke and Montesquieu by allowing for the constitutional exercise of prerogative powers. Because the American social contract mandates a structural and procedural agreement, the record of the courts and the machinations of the political system have established the real, constitutional limits of prerogative power in the American context.

3 Tracing the Outline of the Presidential Prerogative

Beyond the philosophical and structural foundation of the Constitution, there exists a second set of variables that determine the outlines of prerogative powers in the United States. Precisely because the framers of the Constitution left the powers of the executive branch relatively vague, historical practice, precedent, and decisions of court have contributed as much to the profile of presidential prerogative powers as has the written constitution. Even the parts of the Constitution related to the presidency that are very precisely drawn have been molded by circumstance (only less so). Therefore, practical experience has had a relatively greater impact on the prerogative powers of the presidency than it has had on, for example the powers of Congress. This is not to say that Congress is without its own prerogatives. In fact, as will be discussed in the next chapter, Congress has a fairly broad mandate, not specifically sanctioned by the Constitution but accepted in practice by the courts. Nevertheless, the constitutional flexibility of the presidency is without rival in American government. Therefore, an examination of presidential prerogative powers is more likely to take us to the limits of the acceptable in the exercise of emergency powers.

The presidency, because of its structural advantages, is uniquely situated for the exercise of emergency powers. Because of its hierarchical organization and administrative responsibilities, the presidency has an advantage in acting with dispatch and secrecy. Even Locke, who was a great proponent of the sovereignty of the legislature, recognized that the executive had a special responsibility for the exercise of prerogative powers. He wrote in the *Second Treatise of Government*:

> Where the legislative and executive power are in distinct hands, (as they are in all moderated monarchies, and well-framed governments) there the good of the society requires, that several things should be left to the discretion of him that has the executive power: for the legislators not being able to foresee, and provide by laws, for all that may be useful to the community, the executor of the laws, having the power in his hands, has by the common law of nature a right to make use of it for the good of the society in many cases, where the municipal law has given no direction, till the legislative can conveniently be assembled to provide for it.[1]

As a practical matter, he believed, the executive must be free to respond to crisis.

Roughly defined, the executive's prerogative is ideally exercised in response to exigencies that impose time constraints on the ability of government, as a whole, to respond. These prerogatives are limited by procedural constraints and by the Bill of Rights, although certain emergencies may be serious enough to warrant the temporary suspension of individual liberties. Nevertheless, because there is no absolute agreement as to the limits of liberty or about what constitutes a crisis or situation appropriate for the bypass of regular governmental procedures, the outline of the president's prerogative still needs to be established. A review of court decisions and historical precedents should give us a clearer idea of where and in what situations these limits exist.

The courts seem to recognize two general limits to the exercise of prerogative: the political process and the Bill of Rights. The Bill of Rights is the clearest and most unambiguous statement of natural rights in the Constitution. As noted above, however, liberals rarely hold the rights of individuals to be completely inviolate. Certain circumstances and certain values may be promoted at the expense of individual liberties. Therefore, a discussion of the exercise of prerogative powers invariably becomes a discussion of *which* situations may involve the violation of individual rights. While most observers would agree that state survival is a value worth protecting even at the risk of a temporary sacrifice of individual freedoms, beyond that point is controversy. In fact, national survival is rarely at stake in governmental decision making, even in emergencies. There are also certain public goods besides national security in pursuit of which the exercise of prerogative powers may be justified.

Traditionally, the use of prerogative powers was never exclusively restricted to matters involving national security. The king's prerogative extended to policy making related to all aspects of the government's function. As a practical matter it was (and still is) impossible to plan in advance for all the extraordinary situations in which the exercise of prerogative powers might be necessary. Consequently, the limits of prerogative were inexorably linked to the office in government through which those powers were exercised. The king, by virtue of his divine sanction, was "limited" in his exercise of prerogatives by the Supreme Being.

In a republic, the exercise of prerogative powers is delimited by notions of proper representation. The representatives in a constitutional regime have a duty to wield extraordinary powers in a "responsible" manner. What is responsible or irresponsible conduct in a republic is, in part, a function of law and, in part, a function of consensus. The courts and the legislature determine the law. An examination of precedent and historical text establishes the boundaries of consensus. Inasmuch as the most prominent framers of the Constitution subscribed to what later became known as the principle of Burkean representation, prerogative powers came to have a fairly broad sanction in American government.[2]

One of the fundamental rules of civil society, wrote Burke, "is, that no man should be judge in his own cause."[3] Burke argued that in civil society representatives as "trustees" must be allowed to act independently of the control of not only their constituency but of natural law. When constrained by natural law, representatives were in times of peril, powerless. When representatives acted as delegates (or simply ciphers for the public),

Burke believed anarchy and the dominance of faction were the likely result. On the power of government as exercised through representatives, Burke wrote:

> Government is not made in virtue of natural rights, which may and do exist in total independence of it; and exist in much greater clearness, and in a much greater degree of abstract perfection; but their abstract perfection is their practical defect. By having a right to everything they want everything. . . . Society requires not only that the passions of individuals should be subjected, but that even in the mass and body, as well as in the individuals, the inclinations of men should frequently be thwarted.[4]

This notion of representation opens the floodgates for the exercise of prerogative powers in a republic.

While the framers might have found it impolitic, a trampling on the Declaration of Independence, to adopt this Burkean definition of representation, it is this definition that tends to dominate the writings of the framers in the *Federalist* papers. For example, Madison wrote in *Federalist* paper 10: "it may well happen that the public voice, pronounced by the representatives of the people, will be more consonant to the public good than if pronounced by the people themselves, convened for the purpose."[5] Of course, the proper method of selection and the imposition of suitable structures for control would be needed as a safeguard against the excesses of venal representatives. Nevertheless, Madison concluded, representation was vastly preferable to direct democracy in the new republic.

This form of representation may have been appropriate for legislators. The presidency, however, was a special case. Could a single executive be trusted to exercise the Burkean form of representation in a manner that protected individual liberties? This issue had not been settled by the end of the Constitutional Convention. Consequently, from the beginning, the representative character of the presidency was a point of contention.

For the presidency the crucial turning point in the establishment of prerogative powers came with the recognition of the president as Burkean trustee rather than delegate. While George

Washington set some important precedents (not the least of which was the Neutrality Proclamation, about which more will be said later), Thomas Jefferson adopted the broadest, early view of presidential powers. In the case of the Louisiana Purchase, Jefferson wrote in defending his decision to commit to the Purchase:

> The Executive in seizing the fugitive occurrence which so much advances the good of their country, have done an act beyond the Constitution. The Legislature in casting behind them metaphysical subtleties, and risking themselves like faithful servants, must ratify and pay for it, and throw themselves on their country for doing for them unauthorized what we know they would have done for themselves had they been in a situation to act.[6]

The "metaphysical subtleties" to which Jefferson referred were considerations of the role of representatives in a democracy. Broad interpretations of representative rule, such as this, dramatically expanded the possibilities for exercise of prerogative powers.

Jefferson was not alone in promoting activist representation, particularly in the presidency. In *Federalist* paper 70, Hamilton argued that a "vigorous executive" was not only completely consistent with a republican government, but that a strong executive was "essential" to the protection of the community. According to Hamilton, a vigorous presidency would guarantee the steady administration of the laws, the protection of property, and protect against "assaults of ambition, of faction, and of anarchy."[7] Hamilton's intention was to acknowledge the president as a "trustee" whose broad perception of the public interest would allow for the involvement of the chief executive in the entire spectrum of public decision making. How this executive was to be controlled, however, was another question.[8]

For Hamilton, the political system provided the greatest protection against abuse of this sort of extraordinary power. The abusive representative could be turned out of office. Periodic elections provided an incentive for the responsible conduct of representatives.[9] Alternately, appeal to the courts or Congress could provide relief. It seems, then, according to Hamilton, that the primary limitation (beyond the Bill of Rights and natural rights) to the exercise of prerogative powers was a procedural limit. The prerogative powers exercised by the president were confined insofar as they could not be wielded without recourse to due process either in the courts, the Congress, or in the political arena. Nevertheless, regardless of our procedural safeguards, there are moments in our history when the president acts beyond constraint. Congress may not be in session and the courts may be unable to intervene. What force at those times restrains the exercise of the president's prerogative?

The answer to this question is somewhat obscure. Throughout American history controversies concerning the limits of presidential power have been obfuscated by the fact that arguments over specific policies are often expressed in global, constitutional terms.[10] In order to have their way on specific policy issues, congressmen and presidents often lay claim to very loosely defined constitutional authorities. Thus, presidential claims to constitutional powers must be viewed with a healthy skepticism. The potential for hyperbole and abuse associated with those claims are a natural by-product of the competition between the branches created by the separation of powers.

Interpretation of the president's power exist along a continuum that begins at its most restrictive with the constructionism of James Madison and William Howard Taft and ends at its most expansive with the stewardship doctrine of Theodore Roosevelt, Abraham Lincoln, Franklin Delano Roosevelt, and others. From the restrictionist perspective, Taft argued in his memoirs:

The true view of the executive function is, as I conceive it, that the president can exercise no power which cannot be fairly and reasonably traced to some specific grant of power or justly implied and included within such express grant as proper and necessary to its exercise. . . . There is no undefined residuum of power which he [the president] can exercise because it seems to him to be in the public interest.[11]

Apropos of the argument made above, Taft, at the time he wrote his memoirs, was engaged in a bitter political dispute with Theodore Roosevelt. It was not surprising, therefore, that Taft staked out a position diametrically opposed to the one stated by

Roosevelt, which I shall discuss presently. Nevertheless, Taft's reliance on Article 2 grants of power to the executive still left open the possibility of a broad interpretation of the executive's powers under the Constitution. In fact, as a Supreme Court justice, Taft was quite willing to tolerate the wide-ranging exercise of the president's authority in foreign affairs.[12]

A more forthright but much less modern statement of the restrictive view is the position taken by James Madison in the Pacificus-Helvidius debate. In 1793, President Washington proclaimed the United States neutral in the war between France and Britain. Hamilton, writing as "Pacificus," argued that Washington had the power to make such a proclamation even though the United States had existing treaty commitments to come to the aid of France. Madison, writing as "Helvidius," argued that the president had no such power to unilaterally abrogate treaty commitments. Referring to Hamilton's arguments, he wrote:

If the meaning be as is implied by the force of the terms "constitutional powers," that the antecedent state of things produced by the executive ought to have a *constitutional weight* with the legislature; or, in plainer words, imposes a *constitutional obligation;* the writer [Hamilton] will . . . have . . . to reconcile it with his last concession, that "the legislature is *free* to perform its duties according to its *own* sense of them.[13]

In other words the executive could not take actions that would, in advance, obligate the legislature to act. Accordingly, Madison was reluctant in his own presidency to extend the powers of the office.[14]

It is difficult to sustain, as a practical matter, this restrictive view of the office, especially in view of the modern development of air power and nuclear weapons. The possibility of nuclear attack or the vulnerability of Americans traveling abroad make it difficult to constrain completely the president's ability to act in an emergency. However, opinions still differ as to the degree of restrictiveness of the constitutional grants of power to the president. Certainly the incentive exists for presidents to exceed the restrictive view. Not only are presidents likely to be tempted to avoid the frustration of consulting with Congress, historians treat more kindly the presidencies of activist chief executives.[15]

Indeed, Theodore Roosevelt argued in favor of an activist presidency, writing in his memoirs:

I declined to adopt the view that what was imperatively necessary for the nation could not be done by the president unless he could find more specific authorization to do it. My belief was that it was not only his right but his duty to do anything that the needs of the nation demanded unless such action was forbidden by the Constitution or by the laws.[16]

Even this statement of the powers of the president is an over-restrictive interpretation of the presidential prerogatives in practice. Roosevelt still leaves the door open for an interpretation of the Constitution that limits the exercise of prerogative powers to the "parchment barriers" of Articles 1 and 2 and the Bill of Rights. For a more extreme statement of the powers of the executive, we return again to the Pacificus-Helvidius debate. Hamilton stated: "The President is the Constitutional EXECUTOR of the laws. Our treaties, and the laws of nations, form a part of the law of the land. He, who is to execute the laws, must first judge for himself their meaning."[17] The danger in this approach to presidential decision making is that the power to interpret the law often becomes the power to make the law. The Constitution does not always provide a clear guide to its meaning. The Bill of Rights is not completely beyond interpretation, and the countervailing power of the branches is not always well established. In addition, it is not entirely clear at what times the constitutionally mandated governmental process can be held in abeyance in the event of a national emergency. The doctrine of necessity, therefore, is also subject to arbitrary interpretation and, possibly, abuse.

Given the partisanship of the debates in the political branches concerning the proper exercise of prerogative powers, the courts are probably a more reliable source than constitutional text for evaluating the limits of constitutionality of prerogative powers. Somewhat above the fray spawned by the separation of the legislative and executive branches, the courts have adopted a relatively broad view of the presidential prerogative. As a rule, they have avoided providing a "gloss of life" for many precedents by sidestepping intramural disputes between the political branches of government. Nevertheless, the courts have opted on occasion to rule on the limits of the president's emergency powers. While general principles are often difficult to glean from this case law, where the courts have intervened in deciding the proper use of presidential prerogatives, they have established a substantial set of guidelines determining the limits of presidential emergency powers.

There has never been very much debate about whether the president has the right to act in emergencies pursuant to previous congressional authorization. The courts are generally willing to tolerate very broad delegations of power to the president by Congress in military affairs. For example, in 1827, in response to a charge that President Madison ordered the New York State militia mobilized (in 1812) without sufficient justification, Justice Story argued in the case of Martin v. Mott:

We are all of the opinion, that the authority to decide whether the exigency has arisen, belongs exclusively to the President, and that his decision is conclusive upon all other persons. We think that this construction necessarily results from the nature of the power itself, and from the manifest object contemplated by the act of Congress.[18]

This decision was confusing in the sense that the Court refers both to the inherent powers of the presidency and those powers delegated to it by Congress. It was not entirely certain what would be the powers of the president to act without such congressional permission. That question seemed to be answered by the Court in the Prize cases.

In response to the firing on Fort Sumter by Confederates in 1861, President Lincoln ordered, while Congress was still in recess, the blockade of Southern ports and the seizure of cargo (some carried by neutral shipping). Shipowners sued the federal government for the return of their cargo, which had been condemned as prizes of war. The Supreme Court denied the shipowners' appeal. The plaintiffs argued that Lincoln, in acting without the authorization of Congress, had unconstitutionally seized their goods. The Court disagreed and suggested that "the President is not only authorized but bound to resist force by force."[19] Furthermore, between the time that the president ordered the blockade and the Court made its decision, Congress passed a series of resolutions recognizing retroactively that a state of insurrection existed and that the president's actions in the interim (before Congress convened) were proper and appropriate. To the charge that Congress's permission was inappropriately issued after the fact, Justice Grier responded:

> Without admitting that such an act [the recognition that a state of insurrection existed] was necessary under the circumstances it is plain that if the President had in any manner assumed powers which it was necessary should have the authority or sanction of Congress, that on the well known principle of law, "*omnis ratihabitio retrotrahitur et mandato equiparatur*" [the retroactive forgiveness for past actions at the express command of the sovereign power], this ratification has operated to perfectly cure the defect.[20]

This was a modernized restatement of Locke's position on the exercise of prerogative. Prerogative power, of necessity, was to be exercised in response to particular crises rather than specifically at the behest of or pursuant to the authorization of the legislature. If the president exceeded his statutory authority in protecting the nation, congressional authorization could come later. According to the Court, the president had an obligation to respond to crisis even in the absence of authorization.

The Court's recognition that the president's emergency power, without the express permission of Congress, was appropriately wielded in response to crises, invariably introduced a new set of problems. What were the limits to this unilateral presidential authority? How long and in what ways could the president respond to crisis without violating the Constitution? A partial answer to these questions came in 1866. In 1864 a U.S. citizen and resident of Indiana (Milligan) was arrested in that state and tried before a military court on a charge of treason (aiding the Confederacy). He was convicted and sentenced to death by the military court. In his appeal, Milligan's attorneys argued that he could not be tried by military tribunal because the state of Indiana was not part of a war zone (civilian courts were still operating) and, therefore, President Lincoln's suspension of civil law did not apply. The Court agreed with the defendant and ordered the prisoner released. The Court based its decision on two principles. First, since the prisoner was a civilian and the civilian courts were in operation, his right to trial by jury was breached. Second, since Indiana was not a war zone and Congress had not acted to declare it so, the president had no right to declare martial law in that state. There had been times in which Indiana was at risk of invasion. Perhaps, under those conditions, the Court would have permitted the suppression of civil law. However, at the time and in the locale of the arrest no such threat was imminent. Therefore, Milligan was entitled to a civilian trial.[21]

In *Ex parte* Milligan, the Court made a fundamental distinction between the president's powers in war and peace, but other questions remained. For example, if the president's prerogative is limited in peacetime, what are those limits? In general, the Court seems to have confined the president's power in peacetime to a relatively strict definition of the Bill of Rights and the statutory restrictions imposed by the other branches of government.

In 1971, the federal government attempted to enjoin the *New York Times* from publishing the text of the "Pentagon Papers" (an internal Defense Department review of American policies in the Vietnam War). The government claimed that publication of the papers would endanger national security. The Court ruled against the government's request. In his decision, Justice Black writing for part of the majority argued:

In seeking injunctions against these newspapers and in its presentation to the Court, the Executive Branch seems to have forgotten the essential purpose and history of the First Amendment. . . . The word "security" is a broad, vague generality whose contours should not be invoked to abrogate the fundamental law embodied in the First Amendment.[22]

This is not to say that protections of liberty under the First Amendment are absolute in peacetime. The Court, on occasion, has been called upon to make the subtle distinction between the protection of liberty under the Bill of Rights and the legitimate pursuit of national security.

In 1985, the Central Intelligence Agency was sued under the Freedom of Information Act to release the names of researchers involved in studies designed to investigate the effects of brainwashing techniques. The director of the agency withheld the names, citing the National Security Act of 1947, which instructs the director to protect intelligence sources from unauthorized disclosure.[23] The Supreme Court upheld a lower court ruling forbidding the release of the names. Chief Justice Burger stated in his opinion:

The national interest sometimes makes it advisable, or even imperative, not to disclose information that may lead to the identity of intelligence sources. . . . We hold that the Director of Central Intelligence properly invoked . . . the National Security Act of 1947.[24]

Justice Burger took great care to state in his decision that the director was acting pursuant to congressional authorization. Therefore, this case cannot be held as an example of the exercise of the presidential prerogative: the reference to governmental process was preserved, even as the public's right to know may have been infringed.

Nevertheless, there can be situations in peacetime in which true presidential prerogatives are exercised. The most famous example in this regard is the Court's decision in the Steel Seizure case. Even as the Court overruled President Truman's executive order to seize certain steel mills in order to avert a nationwide steelworkers' strike, the Court left open the possibility of the exercise of presidential prerogatives in peacetime. For example, Justice Clark in his decision concurring with the majority wrote:

I conclude that where Congress has laid down specific procedures to deal with the type of crisis confronting the President, he must follow those procedures in meeting the crisis; but that in the absence of such action by Congress, the President's independent power to act depends upon the gravity of the situation confronting the nation.[25]

Presidential prerogatives, therefore, were sometimes to be a function of context rather than statute, even in the absence of formal congressional authorization. Nevertheless, the majority of the Court was of the opinion that the president had misused his executive powers in this particular case.

While there are only a few areas in which the president can exercise prerogative powers in time of peace, the president's powers in time of war are very broad. There are a number of court decisions that justify a broad array of substantial presidential prerogatives in wartime. Arguably, the most famous case in this regard is the Korematsu appeal. In that case, an American citizen of Japanese ancestry challenged an executive order excluding him from his home on the West Coast during World War II. The Court upheld the government's authority to impose legal restrictions on the civil rights of a single racial group.[26] The Court was not clear, however, as to whether the president, alone, had the authority to issue an exclusion order. Nevertheless, there was a suggestion in Justice Black's decision that the president has at least temporary authority to order such a restriction.[27]

In at least two other significant decisions during World War II, the Court approved the exercise of rather broad presidential authority during wartime. In both cases, the president's appointment of special military tribunals to try enemy aliens for war crimes was found to be constitutional. The defendants in both cases argued that their convictions were illegal inasmuch as the special tribunals appointed for their trials violated their rights to trial by jury under the Fifth and Sixth Amendments. In both decisions the Court ruled that since the president exercised wide-ranging powers once Congress had declared war, the appointment of special tribunals was in order.[28] For example, in the case of *Ex parte* Quirin, Chief Justice Stone wrote in his decision: "The Constitution thus invests the President, as Commander in Chief, with the power to wage war which Congress has declared, and to carry into effect all laws . . . [including] defining and punishing offenses against the law of nations."[29] This decision sets an important precedent and also raises another important question concerning the exercise of presidential prerogatives in wartime. It seems that as long as Congress has declared war, the president has access to tremendous powers under the commander in chief clause of the Constitution. The problem is that so few military engagements are likely to be conducted pursuant to a formal declaration of war that it becomes imperative to determine under what conditions these awesome war powers can be brought to bear.

Just what constitutes an emergency that justifies the exercise of these extensive war powers is, then, a matter of great concern. Obviously, if Congress is not required to declare war in order for the president to exercise vast emergency powers, the definition of "emergency" or "war" must be carefully drafted. A key court decision in this regard is the finding of the Court in the case of Woods v. Miller. In 1946, President Truman proclaimed that hostilities related to World War II were ended.[30] In 1947, Congress enacted a law (the Housing and Rent Act of 1947) that limited rents for housing in "defense rental areas." The intent of the law was to compensate for the shortage of housing that existed at the end of the war. In a lawsuit seeking enforcement of the act, Woods brought suit against a landlord (Miller) seeking to prevent Miller from raising rents in properties owned in Cleveland, Ohio (a designated defense rental area). The landlord argued that since the United States was no longer at war, wartime pricing restraints, including the law in question, were unconstitutional exercises of the war power. The outcome of the case depended on the Court's judgment as to whether the war powers still applied. The Court ruled that despite President Truman's proclamation and the agreements ending hostilities signed with Germany and Japan, the consequences of war still existed, if not an actual state of war. As Justice Douglas stated on behalf of the Court:

The legislative history of the present Act makes abundantly clear that there has not yet been eliminated the deficit in housing which in considerable measure was caused by the heavy demobilization of veterans and by the cessation or reduction in residential construction during the period of hostilities due to the allocation of building materials to military projects. Since the war effort contributed heavily to that deficit,

Congress has the power even after the cessation of hostilities to act to control the forces that a short supply of the needed article created.[31]

The crucial point made here by Justice Douglas is that a state of emergency exists as long as the *effects* of the emergency are in evidence. While the Court retains the right to pass judgment as to "whether the war power has been properly employed," the war powers extend beyond formal declarations by Congress. Emergencies exist as a consequence of circumstance and not of proclamation.

The point that the Court seemed to be making in the Woods case is that the exercise of presidential prerogatives is proper under emergency conditions. This, of course, raises the question, What constitutes a "state of emergency"? In 1939, after Franklin Delano Roosevelt had declared thirty-nine "emergencies" in his first six years in office, Congressman Bruce Barton complained: "Any national administration is entitled to one or two emergencies in a term of six years. But an emergency every six weeks means plain bad management."[32] Does an emergency occur simply because the president declares it so? According to the Court's decision in Martin v. Mott (see above), there is little question but that the declaration of states of emergency remains the province of the president. Whether this authority to recognize the existence of a state of emergency is purely an executive authority that can be exercised without the permission of Congress is still in question. In some sense, however, Congress has rendered this question moot. Congress has provided a considerable number of statutes containing broad delegations of power by which the president is authorized to take extraordinary actions by executive order "in case of emergency."[33] These authorities permit the president to take all manner of actions including the seizure of property and the detention of civilians. Because these delegated authorities are so wide-ranging, it is unlikely that the president will ever be without at least some statutory claim to an emergency executive order.

In 1976, in order to check this discretionary prerogative, Congress passed the National Emergencies Act, a law designed to regulate presidential emergency powers. The act requires that the president inform Congress as to the provision of the law under which a state of emergency is being declared. In addition, the act rescinded 470 emergency orders in effect as the result of previous states of emergency declared as far back as the 1930s. Under the law, Congress would also have the power to revoke, by joint resolution (presidential signature required), states of emergency declared by the president.[34] By passing this law, Congress attempted to introduce some sort of formal limits to the president's authority to assume substantial powers through arbitrary declarations of emergencies.

It would be difficult to argue that much has changed as the result of the passage of this law. As we have seen, the courts have been generally reluctant to grant the president, in peacetime, emergency powers not authorized by Congress. Nevertheless, on those occasions in which the president has been forced by circumstance to act without the express permission of Congress (Lincoln and the Civil War, Franklin Delano Roosevelt and the evacuation of Japanese-Americans come to mind as examples), the courts have been relatively tolerant. In addition, as a practical matter, it is difficult to envision anything but the most extreme scenario in which Congress would overwhelmingly adopt a resolution of disapproval (with the two-thirds vote necessary to override a presidential veto). It is unlikely that this law would have prevented the blockade of southern ports during the Civil War or the detention of the Nisei. At the time, Congress approved of both actions overwhelmingly.

The president's prerogative extends into other areas besides war powers. For example, the courts have explicitly recognized that the president has special authority in foreign as opposed to domestic affairs. While the distinction between foreign and domestic affairs is becoming increasingly nebulous, the president is generally granted a great deal of latitude in the conduct of diplomacy and military operations, particularly outside the boundaries of the United States. One of the most important endorsements of the president's special prerogative in foreign affairs was issued by the Supreme Court in the case of United States v. Curtiss-Wright. In ruling that the president had the authority to protect American neutrality in respect to a South American war, Justice Sutherland wrote:

It is important to bear in mind that we are here dealing not alone with an authority vested in the President by an exertion of legislative power, but with such an authority plus the very delicate, plenary and exclusive power of the President as sole organ of the government in the field of international relations—a power which does not require as a basis for its exercise an act of Congress, but which, of course, like every other governmental power, must be exercised in subordination to the applicable provisions of the Constitution.[35]

Unlike the emergency powers exercised by the president, which must be approved if at all possible in advance by Congress, the president's powers in foreign affairs are much less restricted. In a number of cases the courts have recognized the authority of the executive to protect American lives and property abroad without prior congressional authorization.

In 1854, a mob attacked the U.S. consul in Greytown, Nicaragua. A U.S. naval vessel at anchor in the harbor then proceeded to shell the town in retaliation. A resident of the town sued the captain of the ship for damages in a U.S. federal court. The plaintiff claimed that, without congressional authorization, the ship's captain, as a representative of the executive branch, did not have the authority to respond with the use of force. A U.S. circuit court ruled in favor of the defendant (the ship's captain). Judge Nelson argued for the court that "as it respects the interposition of the Executive abroad, for the protection of lives or property of the citizen, the duty must, of necessity, rest in the discretion of the President."[36] "Life and property actions" have been the staple element of armed U.S. interventions abroad, particularly in Latin America, for most of the twentieth century.[37] Because American troops are now stationed and American citizens live and own property all over the world, by virtue of the United States' rise to superpower status, the potential for the exercise of the president's prerogative by virtue of life and property actions has expanded rapidly. The president can always use the presence of American citizens abroad (as did Ronald Reagan in Grenada and Lyndon Johnson in the Dominican Republic) as an excuse to intervene without the prior approval of Congress.

The use of force alone, however, is not the only area in which there is a special reserve of presidential prerogative in foreign affairs. The president also retains important prerogatives in the realm of diplomacy. For example, on several occasions the courts have recognized the authority of the president to enter into binding international agreements without the explicit approval of the Senate. These "executive agreements," while generally unimportant in content, can sometimes entail rather broad-ranging commitments in international affairs.[38] On average, the American government may enter into close to five hundred agreements annually, while in the course of any given year the Senate will consider fewer than thirty treaties.

In 1933, the United States extended diplomatic recognition to the communist government of the Soviet Union. Pursuant to negotiations leading up to the establishment of relations, the United States agreed to act as an agent for the Soviet government in the United States. The Justice Department would help return to the Soviet Union property confiscated in the United States in retaliation for the nationalization of American-held property in the Soviet Union. In 1937, U.S. attorneys sued an American bank for the return of Russian funds on deposit in that bank prior to the 1917 revolt. Representatives of the estate of August Belmont, owner of the bank, argued that the president's agents had no right to seize his property pursuant to the agreement made with the Soviets because, among other things, that agreement did not have the force of law. Nontreaty agreements, Belmont argued, were not legally binding. Thus, the laws of New York State prohibiting the seizure of property applied. The Supreme Court ruled against Belmont's defense and, in so doing, recognized the authority of the president to enter into "executive agreements." According to the Court, these agreements have the force of law but do not require Senate approval. In his decision, Justice Suth-erland wrote:

That the negotiations, acceptance of the assignment and agreements and understandings in respect thereof were within the competence of the President may not be doubted. Governmental power over internal affairs is distributed between the national government and the several states. Governmental power over external affairs is not distributed, but is vested exclusively in the national government. And in respect of what was done here, the Executive had authority to speak as the sole organ of that government.[39]

There are a number of practical reasons that make executive agreements necessary for the conduct of diplomacy. Pursuant to existing laws or treaties, the president or the president's agents may find it necessary to implement parts of a treaty by agreeing to take certain steps not clearly outlined in the text of the treaty itself. For example, the Panama Canal treaty required a number of clarifications in the form of executive agreements. It may also be necessary for the president to enter into executive agreements regardless of the existence of a current authorization.

The courts have ruled, nonetheless, that there are certain for-mal limits to the negotiation of executive agreements. In 1953, a U.S. circuit court found an executive agreement between the United States and Canada to be in conflict with an act of Con-gress. The court ruled that an executive agreement could not be used to alter an existing statute.[40] Furthermore, in 1957, the Supreme Court ruled that international agreements had to "com-ply with the provisions of the Constitution"—the provisions in this case being the individual right to due process under the Fifth and Sixth Amendments.[41] Still, the authority to negotiate exec-utive agreements remains an important diplomatic prerogative.[42]

The presidency also wields its influence over policy making through its participation in the legislative process. As we have shown, the president is required, pursuant to a number of stat-utes, to consult with or report to Congress. The president also formally participates in the legislative process through the use or the threatened use of the veto power. The president's veto power is carefully enumerated in Article 1, section 7 of the Constitution and, therefore, does not qualify as a "prerogative" power in the strictest meaning of the term with one notable exception. The so-called pocket veto in its modern manifestation is a classic case of the development of a presidential prerogative through the process of constitutional construction.

According to the Constitution, "if any Bill shall not be returned by the President within ten Days (Sundays excepted) after it shall have been presented to him, the Same shall be a Law, in like manner as if he had signed it, unless the Congress by their Adjournment prevent its Return, in which Case it shall not be a Law."[43] Accordingly, presidents have traditionally withheld from signature, and thus killed, bills passed at the end of a legislative session. Over the years, presidents have used this provision to "veto" more than a thousand bills.[44] This constitutional provision has produced a number of controversies that are yet to be resolved, such as What constitutes a legislative adjournment in the meaning of the Constitution? May Congress appoint an agent to receive veto messages during recesses, thus obviating the president's power to veto bills in its absence?

In December 1970, President Nixon refused to sign the Family Practice of Medicine Act (S 3418, the bill was passed overwhelmingly by both houses). Because the ten-day period for the signing of the bill expired during Congress' six-day Christmas recess, the president argued that the bill was dead and that he was under no obligation to implement the legislation. Senator Edward Kennedy, one of the sponsors of the bill, filed suit to compel the publication of the bill as a law, arguing that President Nixon had no right to exercise the pocket veto in this case; Congress had not been "adjourned" and the president was, therefore, not prevented from returning the bill to Congress (through the regular veto process). A U.S. court of appeals sided with Senator Kennedy and ruled that the president had not been prevented from returning the bill to Congress and, therefore, the president was obligated to regard the bill as a law.[45] The administration declined to appeal the court's decision.

The Ford and Carter administrations abided by the Court's decision and did not pocket-veto bills during intra- and inter-sessional adjournments. The Reagan administration, however, challenged this practice. In November 1983, Reagan pocket-vetoed a bill (HR 4042) passed at the end of the first session of the 98th Congress. Congressman Michael Barnes and thirty-two other members of the House filed suit in federal court to have the president's pocket veto set aside and the bill published as a law. By the time the Barnes case reached the Supreme Court, the purposes for which the bill was initially adopted no longer existed and the case was "mooted."[46] The Court simply declined to intervene. Consequently, the controversy regarding the pocket veto still remains. President Bush has already indicated that he considers a congressional adjournment of more than three days to be a sufficient time period in which to exercise a pocket veto.[47] It seems likely, therefore, that this prerogative power will continue to be the subject of litigation.[48]

Beyond the president's participation in the legislative process, there are a set of rather amorphous or "implied" powers associated with the president's position as chief executive. In seeing that the laws are "faithfully executed," administrators in the executive branch must make a number of policy-related choices that, in effect, become legislation. There are several situations in which the president may be forced, as chief executive, to exercise authorities not clearly sanctioned by law. For example, Congress may not completely specify in a statute how the executive is to carry out its responsibilities. Congress may pass a law that authorizes certain lump-sum expenditures. In the course of executing that law the executive may take liberties with that expenditure that may not completely conform to congressional intent.[49] Included in the executive's options for the expenditure of funds is impoundment or, within certain limits, the reprogramming of funds originally authorized for a different purpose.[50]

These implied authorities, albeit very loosely defined, were formally recognized by the Court in the case of *In re* Neagle. In that lawsuit, a federal agent (Neagle) was exempted from state prosecution for the shooting of a man who was attempting to assault a Supreme Court justice under the agent's protection. Even though there was no federal statute authorizing Neagle's appointment by the president as bodyguard for the judge, the Court ruled that "any duty of the marshal to be derived from the general scope of his duties under the laws of the United States, is a 'law' within the meaning of the phrase."[51] In other words, it is not necessary for the president (or his agents) to cite a specific statutory authority in order to justify each presidential action.

Accordingly, the executive has often implemented the law or acted on the public's behalf without following the letter of the law. Impoundment authority is the best example of this sort of executive action in domestic affairs. Almost from the beginning, presidents have impounded appropriated funds in order to promote efficiency in government. Because there is generally a delay between the time that Congress approves an appropriation and the time that money is to be spent, the president may find that the expenditure of those funds is not expeditious.[52] In that event, the president may withhold from expenditure legally mandated appropriations only if the effect of that impoundment is to promote efficiency rather than to bring about a policy change.

There is very little judicial precedent to justify any sort of impoundment. In almost every case where it is challenged, the courts have ruled that presidentially impounded funds must be released.[53] Nonetheless, there are occasions when there is virtual unanimity in government about the propriety of a presidential impoundment. In those cases, the president can proceed pursuant to several laws that ostensibly appear to authorize presidential impoundments.[54] These laws, however, cannot constitute direct delegations of impoundment authority to the president. The courts have ruled that Congress cannot delegate its constitutionally mandated authority to appropriate funds.[55] The impoundment authority, therefore, is a true presidential prerogative. It is an implied but not expressed authority that exists beyond the Constitution and the law.

The president's administrative prerogative may even conflict with the ability of Congress to exercise its oversight responsibilities. For example, the president has acted, and the courts have ruled the practice acceptable, to withhold from Congress the records of administrative decision making. The logic behind this protection is that a decision-making process under threat of congressional subpoena would not be open to the expression of all options. What might be said in the heat of a discussion concerning policy making will not necessarily become policy or even be seriously considered. Nevertheless, without privacy, communication between executive officials might be stifled. Consequently, this "executive privilege" extends to all areas of administrative functions. The major exception to this rule is in the case of investigations into possible criminal acts.[56]

There are a number of other components of authority that accrue from the president's role of chief executive in which Congress or the Constitution have not provided a clear guide. As a matter of convenience and practicality the executive branch interprets vague or nonexistent congressional guidelines (informally or formally in the *Federal Register*), or acts independently pursuant to the demands of national security. It would be inaccurate to suggest, however, that even though the Constitution recognizes the president as chief executive, the president has complete control over the implementation of the law. There are a number of reasons that the president's prerogative in the execution of the law is limited.

In 1883 Congress passed the Pendleton Act, designed to replace the spoils system in government with a method for appointing career civil servants on the basis of merit. This attempt to insulate the career civil service from political control resulted in the development of a largely independent bureaucracy that often makes what are, in reality, political decisions beyond the control of elected officials or political appointees.[57] There are a number of other barriers to the effective presidential control of bureaucratic decision making. The sheer size of the bureaucracy makes it difficult to follow the machinations of the implementation of the law.[58] It is very difficult for the president to oversee the implementation of the law at all stages and levels of execution.[59] The fact that political appointees and presidential administrations are relatively transient as compared to the personnel of the permanent bureaucracy makes it difficult for administrative officials to perform adequate follow-up once decisions are made and transmitted from the White House.[60] Moreover, twenty-two of the fifty-six regulatory agencies in the federal government (about 18 percent of all regular federal employees) are independent of presidential control. Their commissioners are appointed to terms not concurrent with the presidential term. In addition, even cabinet departments are thought to be subject to "capture" by constituency groups and to share their loyalty with authorizing and appropriating committees in Congress responsible for agency funding. These "iron triangles" are very difficult for the White House to penetrate and/or circumvent.[61]

What all this means is that the president's prerogatives in the execution of the law, in practice, are limited. This reality extends not only to domestic policy but, to a certain extent, to foreign policy as well. Presidential policies are buffeted by bureaucratic forces at all stages of implementation. One of the most notorious examples of bureaucratic failure to execute a presidential order is the failure of the State Department to effect the withdrawal of obsolete American missiles from Turkey in August 1962. Much to his surprise, President Kennedy discovered that not only were the missiles still in place during the Cuban missile crisis but that negotiations to remove the missiles had been halted. This was so despite a National Security Council Action Memorandum's having been issued directing the State Department to negotiate a removal of the missiles.[62]

In their administration of the law, bureaucratic agencies are forced to interpret broad or unspecific policy guidelines mandated by Congress through legislation. It would not be realistic to expect that Congress will be able to plan in advance for all the problems associated with executing the law on a daily basis. Consequently, most statutes require an ancillary set of regulations governing the administration of the law. The issuance of these regulations is delimited by procedures mandated by the Administrative Procedures Act of 1946, which requires that proposed regulations prior to issuance be exposed to outside review.[63] Nevertheless, administrative regulations often go beyond or are even thought to subvert congressional intent. For example, the regulations of the Occupational Safety and Health Administration (OSHA) are often thought to go beyond Congress's intent in empowering the agency to protect employees without imposing an undue economic hardship on industry.[64]

Presidential control over bureaucratic rule making is an ongoing quest. In an attempt to centralize control of the bureaucracy, the president's staff in the Executive Office of the President (EOP) more than doubled between 1960 and 1972.[65] This effort was temporarily derailed by the Watergate scandal, reducing the size and budget of the EOP accordingly. Nevertheless, in order to improve the quality of their participation in the issuance of federal regulations, recent presidents have begun to develop structures for improving the quality of presidential oversight in this regard. Starting with the Carter administration an attempt was made to increase the amount of control the president has over the issuance of regulations. In 1978, the Regulatory Analysis Review Group (RARG) was established in the EOP to evaluate the economic effects of selected regulations issued by administrative agencies.[66] In 1981 President Reagan ordered that the Office of Management and Budget (OMB), a division of the EOP, oversee all regulations promulgated by executive agencies.[67] Regulations found by the OMB to be unsatisfactory (not withstanding a strict cost-benefit analysis) would then be returned to the agency for reconsideration. As the OMB oversees almost all requests for agency funding before those requests are included in the president's budget, the OMB exercises a powerful influence on agency operations. This effort to control regulation was enormously "successful." Within five months of the issuance of the president's order, there was a 50 percent reduction in the volume of proposed rules and a 33 percent reduction in the size of the *Federal Register* when compared to the same period in 1980.[68]

Finally, I note a prerogative that has been receiving much attention in presidential studies of late. In his insightful book, *The Rhetorical Presidency*, Jeffrey Tulis discusses the transformation of the presidency as reflected through changes in presidential rhetoric.[69] As it was originally conceived, Tulis argues, the presidency was to assert most of its power by virtue of its constitutional base.[70] Increasingly, particularly in the twentieth century, presidents have come to use their office as a "bully pulpit" for the promotion of policies.[71] The frequency and policy content of presidential speeches has markedly increased in this century, particularly beginning with the presidencies of Theodore Roosevelt and Woodrow Wilson.

This exercise of the rhetorical prerogative seems to have manifested itself at two different stages of policy making. First, the rhetoric of the presidency is used as an agenda setter. Presidential communications often become the starting point for the discussion of public policies. For example, President Reagan used the forum of a televised presidential address to introduce the Strategic Defense Initiative. "Star Wars," as that program came to be known, quickly became the focus of public debate and the recipient of billions of dollars in multiyear funding. Second, the rhetoric of the presidency has been used to assert the president's own interpretation of his administrative and emergency powers under the Constitution. For example, President Roosevelt once said in connection with his request that Congress repeal certain portions of the Emergency Price Control Act of 1942:

The President has the powers, under the Constitution and under congressional acts, to take measures necessary to avert a disaster which would interfere with the winning of the war. . . . The American people can be sure that I shall not hesitate to use any power vested in me to accomplish the defeat of our enemies. . . . When the War is won, the powers under which I act will automatically revert to the people—to whom they belong.[72]

This kind of presidential rhetoric provides a justification for and lays the groundwork for future executive actions deemed proper pursuant to the president's own interpretation of the Constitution.

This rhetorical prerogative is taken to its ultimate extreme when the president's rhetoric *becomes* the law. For example, attorneys for President Bush argue that in his "signing statements" (public statements made on the occasion of the signing of legislation), the president spell out an interpretation of the new legislation that is binding on the bureaucracy. In at least one case, President Bush concluded that provisions of a law that he believed were unconstitutional had "no legal force."[73] Presumably, therefore, the bureaucracy and the president himself are under no obligation to enforce these "unconstitutional" sections of the statute even though they were signed into law. This assertion represents an important new foray into areas of unexplored presidential prerogative. Whether this depiction of the president's prerogative will survive, however, remains a matter to be settled in the courts and in the political arena.

The president's prerogative is, therefore, rather substantial. In a national emergency, the president's power is almost absolute, up to and including the suspension of civil liberties. The only real protection against the abuse of power in times of emergency is the consistent judgment of the courts that states of emergency are limited in their duration and initiation. In most cases, the president can only act in an emergency at the behest of Congress. A declaration of war, or similar measure, opens the floodgates for the expansion of presidential powers. In the absence of congressional approval, the president can exercise emergency powers only as long as the crisis prevents Congress and the courts from meeting. Emergencies, then, are a function of circumstance rather than edict. This fact both expands and constrains the president's prerogative power. The president can exercise substantial powers in an emergency without the permission of Congress. However, as soon as the emergency conditions end (*not* when in the personal judgment of the president the emergency is over), the president's power can only be exercised with the concurrence of the other branches of government. The public's liberties are protected in the event of an emergency by the fact that the president does not have, at the same time, the power to exercise emergency powers and to determine, in isolation, when and how long a state of emergency is to last.

The president's prerogative in foreign affairs is much more substantial than in domestic affairs. Primarily, in the protection of the lives and property of American citizens abroad, the president's power, in the short term, is almost absolute. In addition, the president has substantial plenary authorities in the conduct of diplomacy. This includes the authority to enter into binding international agreements without the permission of the Senate. Historical attempts to transfer the president's prerogatives in foreign affairs into the domestic realm have generally run into a literalist definition of the Bill of Rights. "National security" can only be used as a very limited excuse for the violation of individuals' rights in domestic affairs in peacetime.

The president, by virtue of acting as chief executive and legislative participant (through the use of the presidential veto), exercises a variety of "implied" powers or prerogatives that accumulate in the presidency merely as a consequence of the president's position in the policy-making scheme. Ultimately, the chief executive must be responsible for interpreting congressional intent, acting when the Constitution is vague, or conducting government affairs in such a way as to promote efficiency. Very few observers would dispute the claim that the president should, on occasion, fail to carry out a law in order that a law be "faithfully executed." This is particularly true in the case of impoundments. Congress cannot delegate away its appropriation power, but it would certainly approve, and has approved, of executive actions intended to carry out congressional intent and, at the same time, save money. The presidency and its agents also have the responsibility and the privilege of adapting the law to fit the day-to-day operations of government. Congressional intent cannot always be translated into law. Thus, the *Federal Register* becomes, in effect, a reflection of the legislative prerogative as exercised by the executive branch. Recently, the president has begun to develop certain tools that assist in the oversight of agency regulation. In addition, as chief executive, the president retains the right as part of the prerogative power to protect the privacy of the internal decision-making process within the administrative branch by claiming executive privilege.

These powers, taken as a whole, represent a tremendous reserve of authority. The liberties of individuals, however, are protected in this scheme for two reasons. First, the actual range and variety of situations in which the potential exists for the exercise of prerogative powers is limited. National emergencies are rare; Congress is very specific in writing and in overseeing the laws that are most important to its constituents; executive agreements, for the most part, deal with minor affairs; and controversial impoundments and claims of executive privilege are relatively uncommon. More important, individual liberties are protected from the exercise of prerogative because the prerogative power in American government is shared. What would be a contradiction in terms in British government (or most parliamentary governments), the legislative prerogative, is a fact of life in the United States. The fact that the prerogative power is shared in the United States means that Montesquieu's notion (and that of the framers) that the best protection against the abuse of powers is the diffusion of powers, is preserved even in the exercise of prerogative powers.

4 Defining the Congressional Prerogative

Because the concept of prerogative is so often associated with the exercise of powers by a monarch or by an executive branch, it is difficult to envision a set of authorities that could also be considered prerogatives when wielded by a legislature. If we are to define prerogative powers as those powers not explicitly sanctioned by statute or the Constitution but exercised, of necessity, for the public good, there is no reason to assume that Congress lacks such authority. This may be particularly true in American government where the powers of government are at the same time separated and shared. In Britain where the prime minister and her cabinet exercise prerogative powers in the name of the crown, the fact that the cabinet is, at the same time, the executive, legislative, and party leadership means that the concept of a separate, distinct, legislative prerogative cannot exist. However, in the United States prerogative powers are exercised by the federal government as a whole, and because Congress is a separate and distinct entity, prerogative in the United States is unique. Congress plays an independent role in the exercise of state prerogatives. These prerogatives are sometimes limited, with a character distinct from those same powers employed by the executive. Nevertheless, Congress, on its own, can take steps that are in every way as far-reaching as the plenary powers of the president.

Even as the congressional prerogative exists in the United States, it operates under two general constraints. First, because of the exigencies imposed by the conduct of emergency powers, Congress cannot, in practice, take much of a role in initiating a response to most foreign policy and other emergency threats. The presidency, because of its pivotal position in the policy-making process, commands the national agenda not only in emergency but in the day-to-day operations of government as well. Attempts have been made, with varying degrees of success, to find a role for Congress in emergency and diplomatic decision making. The establishment of intelligence committees in both houses, enhanced congressional staffing, the appointment of members of Congress as delegates to treaty negotiations, reporting requirements, the legislative veto, and the reformed budget process all represent attempts on the part of Congress to grasp a portion of the agenda-setting power heretofore (particularly since 1932) exercised largely by the executive. Some of these efforts have been more successful than others. Nevertheless, the difficulty encountered by congressional leaders in establishing a role for Congress in setting the national agenda and responding to crisis is a reflection of the limits imposed by the presidency's structural advantage. The unity, hierarchy, and constitutional role of the executive branch are simply better suited to respond to the demands imposed by crisis.

A second major constraint to the exercise of congressional prerogative is the design of the Constitution itself. With respect to the executive and legislative branches, the Constitution is two very different documents. The powers of the presidency as outlined in Article 2 *seem* much less extensive and *are* much more ill-defined than the powers of Congress as outlined in Article 1. Ironically, however, the specificity of the formal powers of Congress has been more of a restraint than an opportunity for the expansion of congressional power. Because the role of Congress is much more clearly defined in the Constitution, constructionist courts have a greater tendency (and, indeed, an obligation to the original text of the Constitution) to limit the powers of Congress relative to those of the presidency. This pattern of constitutional "construction" has resulted in a gradual expansion of presidential power (relative to that of Congress).[1]

The expansion of presidential emergency and administrative

authority may be an entirely appropriate response, given the threats to national security and the demands placed upon the welfare state in the modern world. However, a number of troubling scandals (including the Watergate burglary and the Iran-Contra affair) in the last few decades have tended to highlight problems associated with the exercise of unrestrained plenary powers by the executive. Consequently, Congress has acted to reinforce its own part in the exercise of emergency and administrative prerogative powers.

There are limits beyond which Congress cannot go in participating in emergency decision making. Time constraints, in particular, make it impossible for Congress as an institution to act in many situations that call for a quick response. In addition, there is a certain degree of license associated with the executive function, such that congressional involvement becomes an actual violation of the executive power or the commander in chief clause. For example, Congress should not have control over the day-to-day disposition of troops in the field. Such involvement would constitute an encroachment upon the president's powers under the commander in chief clause. The same general proposition holds true for congressional involvement in day-to-day administrative decision making and the president's position as chief executive. Therefore, the congressional prerogative in emergency decision making will always be limited unless there is a dramatic alteration of the fundamental structure of American government.[2] There is, however, a distinct exercise of prerogative powers reserved for Congress that accrues from its legislative function.

Fundamental to the legislative function is the responsibility for establishing the law in which hard distributional and ethical choices are made. Regardless of the centrality of the Constitution to the rule of law in the United States, there is room for and, in fact, a need for the interpretation of the constitutionally mandated process of government and the Bill of Rights. Because there is no absolute agreement as to the limits of individual liberty or the power of the branches under the Constitution, Congress is cast in the role, along with the courts, of interpreting the Consti-

tution. In that sense, Congress exercises a "legislative" prerogative in making decisions about how goods are to be distributed
and liberties are to be fixed.

The concept of a legislative prerogative is a departure from
traditional notions of plenary powers. With the executive prerogative, we tend to focus on the "tools" of emergency authority. A
focus on presidential proclamations, declarations of states of
emergency, and of martial law of one kind or another masks the
fact that the executive prerogative is still tremendously limited in
its authority. Nowhere in the mainstream of American political
thought is it argued that the president has the sole authority to
interpret the Bill of Rights. The delegated task of interpreting the
Constitution is, in its essence, a legislative or judicial function.
There may be occasions in which actions must be taken by the
president to impose constraints on individuals. But these occasions can in no way be stretched within the American consensus
to an indefinite time. Time limits must be imposed or legislative
sanction must be elicited in order to legitimize the use of emergency powers by the president. Therefore, the executive prerogative in the United States is less far-reaching than one would
think. The exercise of prerogative by the president is more dramatic and, at the same time, more confined.

By contrast, the legislative prerogative has a more profound
effect on the way society is shaped. In comparison to the instru-
ments used by the president in the application of plenary powers,
the tools that Congress needs to exercise its extraconstitutional
functions are much less intrusive in the short run and much less
well refined. The balance, then, struck between the branches in
the area of prerogative exists in measures of license and execution. Congress and the courts have greater license in their interpretation of the Constitution than does the executive, but the
execution of that license is limited in that Congress and the
courts are unable to enforce their decisions. Just as Congress has
a limited share along with the president of the emergency power,
the president through the use of the veto and the appointment of
judges has a limited share of the legislative prerogative.

In order to carry out its responsibilities pursuant to the legislative prerogative, Congress has appropriated for itself several tools. Most, but not all, of the tools Congress uses to exert its prerogative involve the enhancement of Congress's capability to perform its oversight function. The key to successful oversight for Congress is information. As long as Congress is able to gain access to independent sources of information, it will be able to bring to bear the impressive legislative powers granted to it by the Constitution. Congressional investigatory powers are buttressed by several authorities not specifically outlined in the Constitution but often sanctioned by the courts to be used to the advantage of Congress in the conduct of oversight. Specifically, Congress's subpoena power, authority to hold individuals in contempt of Congress, the empowerment and expansion of committee staffs, the creation of independent congressional investigatory agencies (such as the General Accounting Office), the appointment of special prosecutors for investigating criminal activities (particularly in the executive branch) on an ad hoc basis, and the legislative veto all contribute to Congress's oversight capabilities.

Congress has authorized its committees to conduct independent investigations almost from the moment the Constitution was ratified. In 1792 Congress authorized an investigation into a failed military expedition. By the 1820s, committees of Congress had begun to subpoena witnesses for the purpose of assisting in the creation of new legislation. Court sanction of congressional investigative power came at about the same time. In 1821 the courts ruled that Congress had the right to hold and imprison individuals held in contempt of Congress for refusing to cooperate with committee investigations.[3] The fact that the courts recognized the authority of Congress to cite individuals in contempt of Congress provided impetus for the passage of an 1857 law that provided criminal penalties for refusal to answer "pertinent questions" posed by investigative committees.[4] There were constitutional limits, however, to the imposition of congressional sanctions. In 1881 the Supreme Court overturned a congressional contempt citation on the grounds that Congress cannot pry into "the private affairs of individuals" and that congressional investigations could only be directed in such a way as to contribute to the study of "valid legislation." The Court suggested that, in inquiring into the private affairs of a witness, Congress had attempted to supplant the judicial function and thus deny the convicted individual of rights to due process.[5]

Like the president's emergency prerogative, Congress's investigatory powers seem to be limited by the Bill of Rights and the requirements of due process. However, inasmuch as the Bill of Rights is subject to interpretation, there still existed after 1881 a reserve of congressional investigatory authority yet to be determined. In 1927 a deputy of the Senate, John J. McGrain, arrested the brother of the attorney general, Harry M. Daugherty, who had been subpoenaed and failed to appear before a select committee of the Senate. The defendant, Mally S. Daugherty, petitioned for release, arguing that Congress did not have the power of arrest of its own authority. He was set free by a lower court. The Supreme Court, however, reversed the lower court ruling and Justice Van Devanter, who delivered the opinion of the Court, commented on

two propositions which we recognize as entirely sound and having a bearing on its solution: One, that the two houses of Congress, in their separate relations, possess not only such powers as are expressly granted to them by the Constitution, but such *auxiliary powers* [my emphasis] as are necessary and appropriate to make the express powers effective; and the other, that neither house is invested with "general" power to inquire into private affairs and compel disclosures, but only with such limited power of inquiry as is shown to exist when the rule of constitutional interpretation just stated is rightly applied.[6]

Not only did either house of Congress retain for itself the power of arrest, but the Court's decision also enhanced the general oversight authority of Congress by recognizing "auxiliary powers" outside the Constitution by which Congress could conduct investigations.

But what were to be the limits of Congress's subpoena and arrest powers? Clearly the Court recognized the distinction between the realm of the private and the realm of the public associated with legislative activities. Only the courts could delve into the private activities of individuals. It was not entirely clear, though, how far the limits of legislative inquiry extended. The solution, such as it was, to this question rested mainly on the courts' interpretation of individual liberty under the First and Fifth Amendments.

In the early 1950s the House Committee on Un-American Activities regularly subpoenaed witnesses in order to determine the extent of the "communist threat" within the United States. Witnesses were asked by the committee to disclose their own relationship to the Communist Party as well as to identify others who had a connection with communists and communist front groups. Witnesses often invoked the Fifth Amendment stricture against self-incrimination in refusing to answer questions posed by the committee. However, by relying on the Fifth Amendment, they left unchallenged the implication that present or past membership or association with communist front groups was an illegal activity. In 1954 a witness (Watkins) before the committee decided not to invoke the Fifth Amendment but to challenge the authority of the committee under the First Amendment, claiming that the committee's activities constituted a violation of his freedom of speech. Specifically, Watkins claimed that the committee did not have the right to inquire into the past associations of citizens who were no longer involved in communist activities. Watkins was held in contempt of Congress for refusing to answer the committee's questions. The Supreme Court dismissed the committee's indictment against Watkins. Chief Justice Earl Warren, in delivering the opinion of the Court, argued:

Plainly these committees are restricted to the missions delegated to them, i.e., to acquire certain data to be used by the House or the Senate in coping with a problem that falls within its legislative sphere. No witness can be compelled to make disclosures outside that area. . . . When the definition of jurisdictional pertinency is as uncertain and wavering as in the case of the Un-American Activities Committee, it becomes extremely difficult for the Committee to limit its inquiries to statutory pertinency.[7]

One limit, therefore, to the jurisdiction of a committee of Congress is the original authorization establishing that committee. The investigative activities of a congressional committee pursuant to vague, unspecified authorizations are subject to challenge as a violation of the Fifth Amendment requirement of due process. However, the Court did *not* find the committee's activities to be, as Watkins claimed, in violation of the First Amendment. In fact, the Court was and continues to be very reluctant to restrict the scope of the investigatory powers of Congress.

In 1959, the Supreme Court reviewed the congressional contempt citation of Lloyd Barenblatt, a former college professor who claimed that his First Amendment rights had been violated by the House Un-American Activities Committee. Barenblatt argued that the committee had no right under the First Amendment to inquire about the political beliefs and convictions of witnesses. Such inquiries, Barenblatt argued, were a violation of the freedom of speech. The Court disagreed and upheld Barenblatt's conviction. Justice Harlan issued the opinion of the Court:

That Congress has wide power to legislate in the field of Communist activity in this country, and to conduct appropriate investigations in aid thereof, is hardly debatable. The existence of such power has never been questioned by this Court, and it is sufficient to say, without particularization, that Congress has enacted or considered in this field a wide range of legislative measures, not a few of which have stemmed from recommendations of the very Committee whose actions have been drawn in question here. In the last analysis this power rests on the right of self-preservation, "the ultimate value of any society."[8]

According to this decision, the scope of congressional investigatory activities may be very broad. In fact, as long as the cause of national security is invoked and can be demonstrated to the Court's satisfaction and as long as the committee's authorization is tightly enough drawn, the only protection for individuals subpoenaed to appear before a congressional committee is the shield of the Fifth Amendment. However, in "taking the Fifth," individuals sully their reputations with what constitutes an implied admission (albeit not admissable under the Constitution or in court) of criminal activity. Therefore, congressional investigations have a very large potential for intrusion into the lives of individual citizens.

Congress has gone to great lengths, in recent years, to equip itself to employ this investigatory prerogative. As tools for the exercise of prerogative power Congress uses the legislative veto, reporting requirements, and an enhanced congressional bureaucracy to oversee necessary delegations of power to the executive. Much of the impetus for this enhancement of the congressional investigatory prerogative came during the final stages of the Vietnam War and in the aftermath of the Watergate affair, when there was a certain degree of alarm about the emergence of an "imperial presidency."[9] At that time, Congress took a number of steps designed to redress this perceived imbalance in congressional-presidential relations. Because executive departments have a natural, self-serving institutional interest when supplying information to investigating committees, the main thrust of enhanced investigatory capability was focused on developing an independent information collection capability in Congress. To that end, congressional staffs were expanded, committee staffs were enlarged, new congressional agencies were created (the Office of Technology Assessment and the Congressional Budget Office), existing agencies were enhanced (the General Accounting Office and the Congressional Research Service) and new oversight committees were created (the Budget and Intelligence Committees). Between 1967 and 1987 the personal staffs of members increased 87 percent in the House and 133 percent in the Senate. Committee staffs roughly doubled in size in the Senate and tripled in size in the House during the same period.[10] Overall, between 1967 and 1987 legislative branch appropriations increased at about twice the rate of inflation.[11]

It is difficult to gauge the actual consequences of this reassertion. If presidential "support scores" in Congress are any indication, Congress has been much more assertive in the last decade. Between 1960 and 1974 Presidents Kennedy, Johnson, and Nixon successfully maneuvered through Congress an average of 78 percent of all the initiatives on which they stated a position. By the same standard, Presidents Ford, Carter, and Reagan (1975 to 1986) were successful only 67 percent of the time.[12] While President Reagan retained, in his last two years of office, high (sometimes historic) levels of popularity, his success scores in Congress reached historic lows.[13]

The scores are somewhat misleading with regard to prerogative powers because emergency powers are exercised not in the normal course of the legislative process but in the breach. In emergencies, Congress is only able to exercise its oversight prerogatives when its information collection capabilities remain unobstructed. There is only anecdotal evidence to indicate whether information collection by Congress in times of emergency has improved. By most accounts, Congress is better able to oversee exercises of presidential prerogative.[14] There are, of course, limitations to the quality of its oversight. The courts, as noted above, have recognized the president's prerogatives of executive privilege and national security "holds" on certain intelligence information. There have also been isolated cases of lying to or failing to fully inform the intelligence committees.[15] Nevertheless, congressional oversight has been substantially enhanced even in reviewing the exercise of presidential prerogative.

Beyond the capacity of Congress to review and oversee the activities of the executive—exercises of congressional control that take place after the fact—there remains the unresolved question of the role Congress is to play in emergency decision making itself. The legislative branch, as the primary policy-making organ of government, provides statutory guidelines for the activities of the executive. Nonetheless, when emergencies occur, statutory guidelines may be of little relevance. Congressional involvement in emergency decision making may be truncated at best. Functionally, the role Congress plays in emergency decision making is twofold: passing emergency legislation after the fact and participation in decision making through consultation with the executive.

Congress's legislative prerogative in time of crisis is remarkably wide-ranging and substantial. Inasmuch as governmental activities in the service of "national survival" seems very loosely bound by the courts, Congress is relatively free through statute to restrict the liberties of individuals in case of emergency. For example, in 1942 Congress passed the Emergency Price Control Act, a temporary wartime measure designed to control pricing for commodities and rents. The act authorized the establishment of an Emergency Court of Appeals empowered to exercise "exclusive jurisdiction to determine the validity of any regulation or order of the Price Administrator." In other words, Congress supplanted as an emergency measure the authority of the courts. Under the law a wholesaler (Yakus) was convicted of selling beef above the maximum allowable price. Yakus appealed the conviction, claiming that his right to due process under the Fifth Amendment had been violated. Commenting on the constitutionality of the act, Chief Justice Stone delivered the opinion of the Court:

Our decisions leave no doubt that when justified by compelling public interest the legislature may authorize summary action subject to later judicial review of its validity. It may insist on the immediate collection of taxes. It may take immediate possession of property presumptively abandoned by its owner, prior to determination of its actual abandonment. For the protection of public health it may order the summary destruction of property without prior notice or hearing. It may summarily requisition property immediately needed for the prosecution of the war. As a measure of public protection the property of alien enemies may be seized, and property believed to be owned by enemies taken without prior determination of its true ownership. Similarly public necessity in time of war may justify allowing tenants to remain in possession against the will of the landlord. Even the personal liberty of the citizen may be temporarily restrained as a measure of public safety. Measured by these standards we find no denial of due process.[16]

While the Constitution specifically authorizes Congress to establish the jurisdiction of the courts, and, thus, fully empowered Congress to set up administrative courts under the Price Control Act, Justice Stone's opinion goes well beyond the enumerated grants of power to Congress under the Constitution. According to his decision, there seems to be little or no restraint on the authority of Congress in wartime. The Court's judgment in this regard constitutes an even broader grant of emergency power to Congress than the authority sanctioned by the courts to be exercised by the executive under the same conditions. The executive is at least constrained by the requirement that Congress, whenever possible, authorize extraordinary actions.

The courts have ruled that other components of the Bill of Rights may be waived during an emergency as well. In 1919 the Supreme Court upheld the conviction of a defendant charged with sedition. The defendant had been charged with printing and distributing leaflets opposing the war and the draft. Justice Holmes, writing for the majority, argued: "When a nation is at war many things that might be said in time of peace are such a hindrance to its effort that their utterance will not be endured so long as men fight and that no Court could regard them as protected by any constitutional right."[17] The Court has been generally tolerant of most forms of political expression.[18] However, Holmes regarded the circulation of seditious materials in time of war to be tantamount to shouting "fire" in a crowded movie theatre. Speech that may incite citizens to revolt or exercises of speech that are libelous or inflict actual physical harm on individuals have been restricted by the courts.

Other court decisions have put other liberties guaranteed under the Bill of Rights at risk in wartime. In 1931 the Supreme Court potentially erased the entire spectrum of liberties in discussing actions authorized by Congress that are justified in wartime. In the case of United States v. Macintosh, Justice Sutherland suggested (in writing for the majority in a five to four decision) that almost any constitutionally guaranteed liberty could be temporarily suspended in the pursuit of national survival. Included in his list of liberties that could be "curtailed or denied" were the freedom of speech, freedom of the press, the right to indictment or trial by jury for all (including capital) offenses, protections against the summary seizure of property, and free-market pricing among others.[19] But it was not only in wartime that these liberties could be suspended.

The Great Depression created an economic emergency of unprecedented proportions. All levels of government took action to cushion the effects of economic collapse. The president declared a bank holiday. Congress passed laws supplying funds for mortgagors in arrears with their creditors. The states, in some cases, responded as well. The state legislature of Minnesota passed a law that granted debtors an extended grace period on loans. The Home Building and Loan Association, a Minnesota creditor, filed suit against an exempted debtor, claiming that the debtor should be required to make payment because the state legislature did not have the power under the U.S. Constitution to curtail the property rights of individuals in peacetime by regulating in such a manner (suspending lender privileges) private financial transactions. The law was upheld by the supreme court of Minnesota and that finding was appealed to the Supreme Court of the United States. The Supreme Court faced a dilemma in the sense that to uphold this law would be to expand the definition of emergencies in which the liberties of individuals could be curtailed. In addition, if the Court found that economic emergencies justified the suspension of liberties, would the plenary powers of government (particularly of Congress) be the same in time of economic crisis as they were in time of war?

There was very little question in the Court's decision but that the Depression constituted an emergency worthy of an extraordinary response. But were the prerogative powers exercised in this instance to be as far-reaching as those same powers wielded in time of war? The decision of the Court was not entirely clear in this regard. "Emergency does not create power," wrote Justice Hughes. But "while emergency does not create power, emergency may furnish the occasion for the exercise of power."[20] In Hughes's view, there existed a reserve of power in the Constitution that could be brought to bear if the situation warranted. For example, the war power was not created by war but was unleashed by war.

National survival, therefore, is an overriding consideration in the government's adherence to constitutional law. Certain constitutional "guarantees," including those contained in the Bill of Rights, can be superseded within the limits of the Constitution. This creates a constitutional paradox in that there exists a reserve of power within the Constitution that allows for its own supersession. But what are the limits to power of constitutional government? Does the Constitution sanction *any* activity undertaken by government in pursuit of national survival? In addition, there still remains the question, How far do the limits of the peacetime prerogative extend?

Hughes argued in the same opinion that where the Constitution is so specific as not to permit interpretation (or "construction"), the Court had no choice but to abide by the original text. For example, no more than two senators could be elected from any state; neither could the president be elected by a popular vote without regard to the results in the Electoral College.[21] Thus, the absolute boundary of the exercise of prerogative powers for the legislative branch is the specificity of the Constitution. In Hughes's opinion, "where constitutional grants and limitations of power are set forth in general clauses, . . . the process of construction is essential to fill in the details."[22] Because much of the Constitution is subject to interpretation, including the Bill of Rights, the Court's decision in this case opens the floodgates of prerogative powers in an emergency.

Indeed, taken together, the court cases cited above seem to grant to Congress almost unlimited powers in case of an emergency. The only formal limits to the congressional prerogative are the president's veto power, judicial review, and the existence of a state of emergency. Why, then, do observers tend to focus on the presidency in crisis? This question goes to the root of the problem of defining the exercise of prerogative powers in the American context. As a matter of practicality, the executive is the first line of response in the event of a crisis. Congress can retain for itself all the dictatorial powers of government but, in reality, it cannot exercise those options quickly enough or enforce those decisions once made. Consequently, there is an overwhelming focus on the president's prerogative. Formally, the prerogative powers predominately reside in the legislative branch, but in practice much of the prerogative power in American government is exercised by the president. Even so, Congress has attempted as an ultimate exertion of its prerogative to include itself in the earliest stages of the decision-making process.

Locke went so far as to suggest that emergency decision making was entirely the province of the executive with the legislature to sanction executive emergency decisions after the fact.[23] It is not clear, however, that this Lockean construct transfers very well into the American political system. Constitutional language abounds with references to the participation of Congress in decision making of all kinds, including foreign operations and emergencies. Examples include the Senate's advise and consent authority with respect to treaties and nominations, and the power granted to Congress to declare limited and unrestricted war. However, the extent and methods for the exercise of congressional-presidential consultation in times of crisis are not yet clearly established. Congress has made it plain that it expects to be fully and meaningfully informed in a timely fashion of decisions made in the realm of foreign policy. "Effective" consultation between the legislative and executive branches in the area of foreign policy was defined by one congressional committee as (1) the consultation of relevant committee and subcommittee chairs as well as individual members who are particularly interested in an issue; (2) consultation with Congress in the earliest stages of the policy-making process (before decisions are made); (3) consultation on any issue that will ultimately require some kind of legislative endorsement or commitment of funds; and (4) consultation in a "cooperative" spirit or at least with the recognition that policy is formed pursuant to both domestic and international factors.[24]

Through statutes that authorize some form of a legislative veto, Congress retains for itself a measure of participation in decision making, emergency and otherwise. The "legislative veto" is a vote by Congress (or one house or even a committee of Congress), not subject to a presidential veto, that disallows an action taken by the executive branch.[25] Legislative vetoes were originally devised by Congress to compensate for the massive expansion of executive authority in the aftermath of the passage of New Deal legislation in the 1930s. To the extent that Congress was forced to delegate substantial authority to the executive branch (in order for the president to implement massive new programs), the legislative veto was conceived of as a device for democratic control. Through the legislative veto Congress could retain for itself a measure of control over the day-to-day operations of the executive even as, in the aftermath of the New Deal, government took on a whole new range of responsibilities.

The earliest legislative vetoes dealt mainly with administrative matters internal to the executive branch. For example, in 1939 the president was given the power to reorganize the executive branch subject to a legislative veto.[26] Later, the use of the legislative veto was extended beyond the reorganization authority to ensure congressional involvement in some of the most important functions of the executive branch. By the early 1980s there were in statute more than two hundred legislative vetoes regulating everything from the decision to use force, to arms sales, to the making of immigration determinations. In addition, there were countless informal arrangements whereby executive agencies agreed to review administrative policy with committees of Congress prior to implementation.

In 1983 the Supreme Court reviewed the constitutionality of a one-house legislative veto provision in which the House of Representatives reversed an immigration determination made by the attorney general. The House's action was appealed in the courts. In INS v. Chadha, the Court declared the one-house legislative veto provision in the Immigration and Naturalization Act unconstitutional.[27] Justice Burger argued that such legislative veto provisos violated the bicameral and presentment requirements of the Constitution.[28] In a departure from customary practice, Justice Burger's decision went well beyond the statute in question seemingly to invalidate all forms of the legislative veto. Subsequent court decisions appeared to confirm the Supreme Court's invalidation of all legislative vetoes.[29] Nevertheless, congressional committees continued to enter into informal arrangements with the executive branch that were in every sense functional legislative vetoes. In addition, Congress passed into law well over one hundred provisions after 1983 that could be considered statutory legislative vetoes.[30]

Legislative vetoes continue to appear in laws because they are the product of a compromise that serves the interests of both the executive and legislative branches. As a practical matter, Congress must delegate broad authority to the executive. Administrative departments need a certain degree of flexibility in order to carry out broad delegations of power. Congress, however, would prefer to retain for itself a role in making day-to-day decisions concerning the execution of the law. The legislative veto is a convenient tool that guarantees relative flexibility in the administration of the law and, for Congress, a modicum of control. The fact that the executive and legislative branches continue to use the legislative veto despite the courts' ruling is an indication of the limits of the courts' practical authority and foresight. The courts' prerogative, too, is limited. Judicial decisions are constrained, as we shall see, by a political system that will simply not support the enforcement of largely unpopular or impractical rulings.[31]

In addition to legislative vetoes, congressional participation in executive decision making is enhanced by reporting requirements. The president and administrative agencies are required by law to make literally hundreds of reports to Congress every year. For example, the Hughes-Ryan Amendment to a 1974 foreign aid bill required that covert actions conducted by or on the behalf of the C.I.A. were to be reported to "the appropriate committees of Congress."[32] With the establishment of the intelligence committees in both houses in 1976 and 1977, Congress often participates as a clearinghouse for covert operations.[33] Many other reporting requirements in the area of diplomacy, economic, and other areas of domestic policy round out a very close relationship between Congress and the administrative state.[34] It should also be pointed out that besides the statutory requirements, there are a myriad of informal relationships that exist between congresspersons, congressional committees, and the executive branch. Frequently, members of authorizing and appropriations committees have a very close personal and, thus, consultative relationship with their counterparts in the permanent bureaucracy.[35]

Besides required reports and daily contacts with administration officials, Congress has a number of *internal* procedural tools at its disposal for the extension of the legislative prerogative. These procedural tools are a powerful resource in Congress's attempt to counter the president's rhetorical advantage in setting the national policy agenda. Congress is fully capable of adapting its own internal deliberation process for the purpose of promoting its own agenda. For example, pursuant to the 1974 Budget and Impoundment Control Act, Congress established a reformed budget process designed to produce a "congressional budget" that is separate and distinct from the president's own budget submission.[36] While this effort has been less than successful (the president's budget is still largely the baseline for debate), it is an example of how Congress can use its own internal decision-making process to set policy. Another, more successful tool for the assertion of the legislative prerogative is the omnibus approach to legislation. A piece of omnibus legislation is a bill that contains the authorization or funding for a number of different, disparate projects. Because there is no constitutional provision for a presidential line-item veto, the president is forced to sign or veto an entire legislative package. Thus, in the case of omnibus legislation, what the president wants in terms of legislation is held hostage to those portions of the legislation he opposes. By virtue of the omnibus approach to legislating, Congress can force the president to sign into law legislation with which he disagrees.[37]

Finally, congressional participation in executive decision making has also been enhanced by the actual participation of members of Congress in diplomatic negotiations and as members of U.S. delegations to international organizations. Members of the Senate are regularly included in treaty negotiations, and at least one member of the Foreign Affairs Committee or of the Foreign Relations Committee is made a delegate to each new session of the United Nations. In addition, congresspersons are often appointed to serve on bipartisan commissions and negotiating teams that are charged with the responsibility of short-circuiting the legislative process by working out agreements between the president and Congress in advance of the adoption of legislation. For example, in advance of President Bush's submission of a budget plan to Congress in 1989, congressional negotiators worked out a compromise budget plan with White House representatives for fiscal year 1990 that both abided by the Gramm-Rudman anti-deficit law and incorporated the concerns of congressional leaders and the president. These annual, informal budgetary negotiations show every sign of becoming a regularized, institutionalized process.[38]

The difference between the exercise of prerogative powers in domestic as opposed to foreign policy is not so clearly drawn in the case of the legislative prerogative. The president as commander in chief and chief executive has an obligation to respond to extraordinary circumstance as a sort of "first line of defense." There is no structural, procedural, or political alternative to a presidential response in times of emergency. Congress, however, may choose to abrogate or delegate its responsibilities by relying exclusively on the unchallenged actions of the executive. Congressional participation is conditioned much more directly by constituency concerns and the internal dynamics of the institution. To a certain extent, Congress has traditionally shied away from intervening in foreign-policy issues that may not deliver, for individual members, domestic political rewards.[39] Recently, however, because of the increasing interrelationship between international and domestic politics, scholars have begun to talk about "intermestic" issues, or matters traditionally identified with foreign policy, in which Congress takes (in the interest of delivering good constituency service) an active interest.[40] As international trade, for example, becomes a much more important influence on the American economy, we should expect Congress to exercise its legislative prerogatives more actively. A unique characteristic of the legislative prerogative, therefore, is the varying degree to which Congress asserts itself in foreign affairs as a function of institutional will. The degree of parochial interest generated by an issue partially delimits congressional exercises of prerogative powers.

While the attraction of intermestic issues draws Congress into the vortex of foreign policy making, other institutional character-istics of Congress work against the active exertion of the congres-sional prerogative. Besides the fact that the separation of the two houses of Congress still stimulates an active and vital division be-tween members of the legislative branch, congressional reform also tends to divide the houses of Congress against themselves. The decentralization of power in Congress (particularly in the House of Representatives) that resulted from reforms adopted by the Democratic Party Caucus in the early 1970s in some ways eroded the ability of Congress to organize itself for the assertion of its prerogatives.[41] However, decentralization as an influence on the ability of Congress to assert itself should not be overempha-sized. "Subcommittee government" did not have the effect of di-rectly enhancing the power of the president.[42] The impact of subcommittee reforms on the distribution of power in govern-ment has been much more complex.[43] Congress has always been thoroughly capable of asserting itself when there existed within the institution some sort of consensus. If the performance of Congress in the waning days of the Reagan administration is any indication, the ability of Congress to assert itself has remained intact regardless of intrainstitutional reforms.[44]

Congressional prerogative powers encompass a broad assort-ment of authorities that can best be described as legislative pre-rogatives. In general, Congress and the Court together interpret portions of the Constitution that are not completely delineated. The congressional prerogative permits the ongoing process of constitutional construction to continue as the nation adjusts to circumstances such as changes in the international environment, changes in the global interests and capabilities of the state, and changes in technology. The framers never conceived of the modern power and reach of the United States as a superpower. Current conditions frequently require that Congress exercise prerogative powers in adapting the processes of government to the requirements of a superpower and the welfare state. Congress also interprets the Bill of Rights in the modern context. Freedom of speech issues such as federal elections laws, regulation of the media, and citizen access to governmental information are all subject to congressional legislative activity. States' rights, civil rights, and civil liberties have all been the focus of congressional attention.

Congressional authorities in wartime are also extremely broad. Under certain conditions, the Supreme Court has upheld legislation that permits the seizure of property, the forced removal of citizens from their homes, the curtailment of the freedoms of speech and press, curtailment of the right to due process and trial by jury. The legitimate pursuit of national survival seems to encourage the entire gamut of governmental powers. That these authorities can be exercised in our society without the loss of governmental legitimacy is a testament to the flexibility of our Constitution that Bagehot was so willing to deride. The courts approve as *constitutional* the use of extraordinary authorities in time of emergency. This leaves us to ponder the possibility that in the exercise of prerogative powers the Constitution of the United States exists as something larger, broader, and more ephemeral than the document that sits in the archives in Washington, D.C.

Congress has developed a number of tools to assist in its exercise of the oversight prerogative. An entire separate and distinct congressional bureaucracy has grown up around the Capitol building. These agencies and enlarged staff are dedicated (when they are not doing casework) to the provision of an independent source of information for Congress to assist in its oversight investigations. Various committees in Congress have been constituted to do little more than oversee the activities of the executive branch, particularly in its conduct of budgetary and national security affairs.[45] Procedural reforms such as the legislative veto (in both its formal and informal manifestations), reporting requirements, the provision for independent special prosecutors,[46] and expanded congressional subpoena power have all contributed to the expansion of the congressional prerogative. The much-feared "imperial presidency" of the 1960s and 1970s has been replaced by a healthy (in the eyes of many) congressional-presidential balance. Congress may occasionally abdicate its oversight responsibilities, as it did between the end of World War II and the Watergate scandal, but a recurrence of congressional complaisance seems unlikely given the heightened political and parochial significance of issues involving the international economy, the bureaucracy, and the budget.

The framers were correct in assuming that a constitution could not be *written* that would provide for every contingency.[47] The current dynamism of the exercise of prerogative powers in American government shakes our understanding of constitutionality to its foundations. With the frank admission that there exists a realm of authority outside the formal, written constraints of the Constitution, we are called upon to reconsider fundamentally the meaning of constitutionality in the American context. Specifically, we must consider the possibility that if the exercise of prerogative powers in their most extreme manifestations is constitutional, the American constitution exists less as a written document and more as what we tend to identify as a social contract.

5 Exploring the Judicial Prerogative

As the forum of last resort, the judiciary in the United States has established itself as a major player in the policy-making scheme. It is not entirely clear that the framers intended the courts to play such a crucial role in adjudicating disputes between the branches. In fact, the framers had little to say about the courts. The Constitutional Convention spent only parts of three days debating the status of the courts, and much of that time was devoted to a discussion of states' rights. The power of the courts to overrule acts of Congress and the president was never clearly established, which led to confusion concerning the role of the courts. Hamilton seems to have been of two minds in regards to the judiciary. In some passages in the *Federalist* papers he stated that the courts would have the power to declare bills passed by Congress unconstitutional. At other times, his endorsement was not so clear. Madison, on the other hand, seemed unenthusiastic about the power of the courts, not so much because the power of judicial review constituted a threat, but because the power of judicial review seemed not enough to protect individual liberties. Jefferson, always the pragmatist, found the Court at first acceptable and then abhorrent (when Justice Marshall chose to use the bench as a forum to scold the Jeffersonian presidency). One thing is certain, however: the powers of the Court are mostly implied and are, therefore, primarily prerogative powers. Of all the branches of government, the judiciary is the greatest beneficiary of the expanded American constitution.

By the time of the American Revolution, an extensive legacy of judicial precedent and theory had been established both in the colonies and abroad. Before the establishment of parliamentary sovereignty in England, the notion that there existed a higher law that governed beyond the rule of kings meant that sometimes common-law standards could be used by English courts to overrule the acts of Parliament or even the acts of the monarch. In the early seventeenth century, English courts could not legislate but they could rule the exercise of the ordinary prerogative by the king or a legislative act of Parliament to be null and void. As Sir Edward Coke, who served as chief justice in England until 1616, argued, "in many cases, the common law will control acts of Parliament and sometimes adjudge them to be utterly void; for when an act of Parliament is against common right and reason. . . . the common law will control it, and adjudge such act to be void."[1] Coke's decision in the Bonham case was cited by English jurists until the time of the American Revolution. American legal scholars of the colonial period were certainly schooled in Coke's theory of judicial review and, thus, were ready to envision a judiciary with powers to challenge the supremacy of the legislature.[2] However, by the time of the American Revolution, English law had already moved away from Coke's conception of judicial review in the belief that the power of the courts to declare the acts of Parliament unconstitutional was a violation of the sovereignty of the legislative branch.[3] After all, for the House of Commons to surrender its sovereignty to the courts would be to surrender the principles of the Glorious Revolution and the rights of the classes represented in the Commons.

During the prerevolutionary period, the courts in the American colonies acted more as an extension of the English Crown than did the courts in Britain. One of the major complaints against the colonial rule of George III involved the tendency of the courts in the colonies to overrule, as an exercise of the king's prerogative, the acts of colonial assemblies. By contrast, since the time of the Glorious Revolution in England, judicial independence had been guaranteed by the life tenure of judges, who served not at the pleasure of the king or Parliament but so long as they maintained good behavior. Furthermore, the courts in Britain were forbidden to overrule the acts of Parliament. In the colonies, however, because judges served at the pleasure of the king's ministers, the courts became a tool of oppression. It was widely held by the king's courts that the king and Parliament could overrule the acts of colonial assemblies. For example, in 1761 the General Court of Massachusetts ruled that "every act we make, repugnant to an act of Parliament . . . is *ipso facto* null and void."[4] So repulsive was this subservience of the colonial courts to the king that in no revolutionary state constitution did the judiciary serve at the pleasure of the executive.[5]

In most early state constitutions the judiciary served at the pleasure of the legislature. For example, in most state constitutions, the governor surrendered to the legislative branch the traditional executive authority to appoint judges. In addition, in most states, the jurisdiction and the composition of the courts was almost exclusively set by the legislature. This emphasis on legislative control of the judiciary reflected the heavy emphasis in revolutionary-era constitutions and the Articles of Confederation on the sovereignty of the people as expressed through legislatures. Also, inasmuch as the judiciary was regarded as agent of the executive branch, the rejection of judicial independence reflected the rejection of executive power in general. The rights of citizens were to be protected by the legislature and, in many cases, a bill of rights written into many state constitutions. There was, however, countervailing influence at work.

In several instances prior to the Glorious Revolution, the courts in England had become a forum of appeal against the violation of common law by the Crown or Parliament. In the colonies, as well, the courts in some cases had been sympathetic to the colonists' cause and had begun to protect citizen rights against the Crown. For example, in 1766 a Virginia county court held the Stamp Act unconstitutional.[6] Because the courts in the colonies had become, in some cases, centers of resistance, it was just as easy to argue that an independent judiciary was important for the protection of individual liberties.[7] Consequently, when the Constitutional Convention convened, there was no general consensus as to the potential status of the courts. What the convention eventually agreed to, Article 3, was a compromise of sorts and, also, a construct of uncertainty similar in its lack of clarity to the empowerment of the presidency under Article 2.

Among the greatest defects of the Articles of Confederation was the absence of provision for the imposition of a national standard of individual liberties. The obvious emphasis in the Declaration of Independence on the natural rights of man was subverted because the federal government under the Articles had to act through the states as intermediaries in order to enforce the law. Most state governments had been respectful of citizens' rights during the interim between the end of the Revolution and the Constitutional Convention, but there had been some notable exceptions. Although America, at the treaty negotiations in Paris, had made promises to protect the property and rights of the king's loyalists in the colonies, widespread looting and assault (a postrevolutionary favorite was tar and feathers), sometimes with quasi-official sanction, was conducted against citizens who had supported the king. In western Massachusetts so-called regulators representing debtors' claims rampaged against courts and administrators; these actions culminated in Shays's Rebellion. In other states, citizen action of the kind that occurred in the waning days of colonial rule continued to be the norm.[8] Not only were mobs and citizens' committees likely to resort to violence to press their claims, but even state legislatures began to go beyond their revolutionary mandates.

Among the complaints leveled at state legislatures were charges that property rights had been violated and that the volatility of the state assemblies made it impossible to conduct private affairs with any reasonable assurance that the laws regulating exchange would not change at a moment's notice. Representative government, in the opinion of many, had become a form of democratic despotism. Many American intellectuals came to the conclusion that the usurpation of the executive and judicial function by the legislatures had made it impossible for citizens to receive due process in redress of their claims. According to this view, the mistake of most state constitutions was assuming that society would be protected against the abuse of legislatures by a social contract.[9] Citizens would simply agree among themselves to respect the rights of individuals pursuant to natural law. However, theorists of the social contract such as Rousseau and Locke, had given too little consideration to the problems of factionalization in a democratic society. Perhaps contract theorists had too much faith in the character of mankind, in that they expected in a contractual society the submergence of petty, personal ambition. The social contract, however, was too fragile a structure upon which to rest the freedoms of individuals. Hence, the framers went beyond social-contract theorists to look for a structural, rather than sociological, basis for the control of government. It was not possible in the absence of countervailing forces or institutions for the government to control itself.

Montesquieu's *Spirit of the Laws* provided answers to some of the framers' questions. Montesquieu never resorted to the social contract or the general will as devices for the control of government. The legislature alone could never be relied upon to respect the rights of individuals. Thus, in addition to the establishment of a strong countervailing executive branch, Montesquieu also placed a certain degree of emphasis on an independent judiciary. The judicial power was to be a distinct, independent function. Montesquieu wrote:

There is no liberty, if the power to judge is not separated from the legislative and executive powers. Were the judicial power joined to the legislative, the life and liberty of the citizens would be subject to arbitrary power. For the judge would then be the legislator. Were the judicial power joined to the executive, the judge could acquire enough strength to become an oppressor.[10]

The judicial power, Montesquieu believed, was to be for the purpose of punishing crime and passing judgment upon disputes arising among individuals.[11] Thus, the judicial power was to deal primarily with the rights of individuals. For the framers, however, this was not a perfect fit. They were forced to adapt the concept of an independent judiciary that was to protect the rights of individuals to a set of special conditions existing under the new Constitution. How could the courts, particularly the federal courts, protect individual liberties and, at the same time, respect the sovereignty of the states and the independence of the other branches of government?

There was almost universal agreement in the Convention about the need for a federal judiciary. Both the New Jersey and Virginia plans provided for some kind of federal bench. However, inasmuch as the new Constitution was established to impose the authority of a central government over the thirteen states, the judiciary would have to be adapted to the notions of federalism. In order to protect individual rights of all citizens and to superimpose the authority of the central government over the states, federal courts would have to have the power to overrule the edicts of state courts and legislatures. This was a major point of contention in the Constitutional Convention. On Wednesday, 18 July 1787, the convention took up the question of the appointment and empowerment of the federal judiciary. Predictably, there were objections to the imposition of the courts' authority over the states. In particular, there were vehement objections to Resolution 16, which stated "that a Republican Constitution and its existing laws ought to be guaranteed to each State by the United States."[12] So forceful were the objections to the imposition of a universal standard by a central government, that the resolution had to be amended to delete the guaranteed enforcement by the federal government.[13] The convention did adopt, however, Resolution 7 which established as binding, "the respective laws of the individual states to the contrary notwithstanding," treaties and "legislative acts of the United States, made by virtue and in pursuance of the articles of the union." This resolution, however, was only adopted after the rejection of a resolution that would have given the federal government "the power of negativing laws of the States."[14] The substitute motion, in deleting any reference to the centralized authority of government, was carefully crafted to leave out any mention of state constitutions as being subject to federal pronouncements. This was hardly a ringing endorsement of federal, much less judicial, review of state pronouncements.

In addition to the consideration of states' rights, in constructing the judiciary, the convention also had to grapple with the problem of protecting individual rights within a constitution that did not contain a bill of rights. Since the emphasis in the new Constitution was on the establishment of *mechanisms* rather than *standards* for control, the only way a judicial branch could carry out its primary function of protecting individual liberties would be to have the power to pass judgment on the actions of other parts of the government. The power of judicial review in this Constitution would have to extend to overruling the acts of Congress and the president. This is a logical, if not explicit, conclusion to be drawn from the construction of the Constitution absent the Bill of Rights.

That the judicial branch was to be independent was generally noncontroversial. Judges were given life tenure and received a salary that could not be diminished during their time in office.[15] That the judiciary was to have the power to overrule the other branches was much more problematical. Part of this confusion stemmed from the fact that, initially, the powers of the judiciary were perceived of as an adjunct of the executive power. After all, the courts in England, and particularly in the colonies, had served at the pleasure of the king. Furthermore, to the extent that the executive function was thought to comprise both the power to interpret the law and to administer the law, the courts in their interpretive capacity were believed to participate in government as an executive institution. Consequently, much of the constitutional convention was predisposed to establish a formal relationship between the judicial and executive branches (as a counterweight to the legislative).

On Saturday, 21 July 1787, James Wilson proposed (with James Madison seconding the motion) that "the supreme National Judiciary should be associated with the Executive in the Revisionary [veto] power."[16] Madison considered this motion to be of "great importance," inasmuch as the association of the judiciary and the executive would both give the judiciary added protections against the encroachment of the legislature and would bolster the veto power of the executive. The supporters of this motion were particularly concerned about the recurrence of abuses, at the national level, that had occurred in the state legislatures under the Articles of Confederation. The inclusion of judges in a kind of "council of revision" would lend legitimacy to the negation of acts of Congress. Opposition to the motion, however, was very strong and was best summarized by Nathaniel Gorham when he argued:

There are two main objections against admitting the Judges to share in it [the veto] which no observations on the other side seem to obviate. The first is that the Judges ought to carry in the exposition of the laws no prepossessions with regard to them. Second, that as the Judges will outnumber the Executive, the revisionary check would be thrown entirely out of the Executive hands.[17]

The motion was then narrowly voted down (ayes, 3; noes, 4; divided, 2). The argument that giving the judiciary a hand in using the veto power would violate the separation of powers seemed to carry the day. Missing in this debate, however, was an explicit objection to the power of an independent judicial review. The framers had overlooked the obvious. Or *was* the power of judicial review obvious? Certainly the reaction of members of the convention to the eventual development of judicial review indicates that they had not planned for the consequences of leaving the powers of the judiciary ill-defined.

As it turned out, Article 3, which empowers the courts, makes some rather cryptic references that could be construed to empower the Court to overrule the acts of Congress and the states. The Article mentions only one court specifically, the Supreme Court, but fails to elaborate on the composition, size, procedure, or internal organization of the federal courts. The jurisdiction of the courts is spelled out in section 2 but is again very vague. The judicial power extends to "all cases, in law and equity, arising under this Constitution, the laws of the United States, and Treaties made, or which shall be made, under their authority."[18] Functionally this means that the federal courts have jurisdiction over diplomatic cases, cases in maritime law, cases to which the United States is a party and cases in which disputes exist between citizens of one state and citizens of another state or nation. Certainly in combination with Article 6, clause 2, which establishes the hierarchy of law in the United States (the supremacy of the central government), the Constitution is fairly clear in establishing the supremacy of the courts in ruling on the constitutionality of state or local issues.[19] But it is not clear wherein lies the jurisdiction of the court in disputes over the constitutionality of acts of Congress or the president. If the federal government is supreme and the Congress as the legislative branch is first among equals, could the courts subvert the popular will by reversing the acts of Congress?

Alexander Hamilton certainly believed that the Supreme Court was to become the great and final arbiter of constitutional disputes. In *Federalist* paper 78 he wrote:

It is far more rational to suppose that the courts were designed to be an intermediate body between the people and the legislature in order, among other things, to keep the latter within the limits assigned to their authority. The interpretation of the laws is the proper and peculiar province of the courts. . . . the Constitution ought to be preferred to the statute, the intention of the people to the intention of their agents.[20]

While this seems to be a fairly clear commitment to the modern concept of judicial review—including the power of the courts to judge the suitability of the actions of coordinate branches—it is, for the time, a relatively rare commitment. Madison, for example, was not willing to go beyond a discussion of the judicial power to review the actions of state governments.[21]

In the earliest days of the republic, judges, because they were perceived of as agents of the executive, were employed by presidents for various administrative tasks. Washington solicited Chief Justice John Jay's advice on proposed legislation. Jay also, while a member of the Court, traveled to Britain as Washington's special ambassador. Similarly, a few years later, Justice Oliver Ellsworth was sent on a diplomatic mission to France by John Adams. To further obscure the distinction between the judiciary and the executive, Jay served briefly as both chief justice and Washington's secretary of foreign affairs. Later, John Marshall served as both chief justice and secretary of state for several weeks after the election of Thomas Jefferson.[22] This use of the judiciary for administrative tasks created a tension that recalled Nathaniel Gorham's objection to the Council of Revision resolution in the Constitutional Convention. The independence and, more important, the impartiality of the judicial branch was called into question when it operated as an adjunct of the presidency. Consequently, the judiciary began to withdraw from its relationship with the executive. First, as we shall see, the Court began to decline presidential requests that it participate in the executive function. Second, the Court began to assert a prerogative peculiar to the judicial function: the power of judicial review.

It was inevitable that in the new government Congress would probe the limits of the Constitution. In 1792 Congress passed a law to settle pension claims against the federal government. Under the law the courts were to pass judgment on individual claims with the secretary of war and Congress to act as final courts of appeal. The reaction to this law in the courts varied from one locale to another. The courts in New York executed the law but the circuit court in Pennsylvania, headed by James Wilson, refused to proceed under the act in any capacity. Wilson's primary objection to the law was that it diminished the powers of the judiciary by providing for litigants a judicial appeal to the political branches of government. Ultimately, a petition was filed with the Supreme Court to force the courts in Pennsylvania to grant a pension to a particular claimant. The Court delayed a decision on the case until the next session of Congress, at which time an alternate method of granting pensions was provided.[23] In addition to asserting its independence, the Court for the moment had avoided a constitutional controversy.

Several other cases were brought before the Court prior to 1803 that could have been vehicles for the establishment of the principle of judicial review. However, in each instance the Court was reluctant to touch off the storm of controversy that would come of overruling an act of Congress.[24] This caution was well justified; the courts, lacking a law-making or enforcement capacity, were in a very precarious position in the early days of the republic. Under the Articles of Confederation, state legislatures had simply overwhelmed the power of their courts by manipulating the tenure or jurisdiction of the judiciary.[25] Thus, when the courts in the new republic constituted a threat to the prerogatives of the Congress, of the president, or of the states, members of Congress (many of whom were past members of state legislatures) reverted to their old methods.

In 1799 the Eleventh Amendment was ratified. Under the amendment, a state cannot be sued in a federal court without its own express consent.[26] This amendment arose as a consequence of a dispute in 1793 in which two citizens of South Carolina sued the state of Georgia in the federal courts to collect a debt.[27] When the Supreme Court agreed to hear the case, the Georgia House of Representatives was so irate that it made it a felony punishable by death (without benefit of clergy!) to attempt to enforce the Supreme Court's decision in the case. Other states were also alarmed by this broad interpretation of the federal courts' jurisdiction that would put the debt-ridden states at risk of a barrage of claims emanating from the federal bench. In 1794 the Eleventh Amendment was proposed in Congress; five years later Chisholm v. Georgia had the distinction of being the first Supreme Court case overturned by a constitutional amendment.[28]

In the election of 1800 the Jeffersonian Republicans took control of both political branches of government. Prior to the election, however, one of the last acts of the Federalist Adams administration had been to expand the number of federal district courts from seven to twenty-three. Naturally, the new benches were filled by Federalist judges. Consequently, when the Republicans took office they faced a hostile judiciary protected by life tenure. At Jefferson's suggestion the Republicans immediately moved in Congress to repeal the establishment of the new district courts. The Republicans believed that while the new Federalist

judges could not be removed by impeachment, they could be removed if their offices were abolished. After all, the Constitution
gives Congress the power "to constitute tribunals inferior to the
Supreme Court."[29] The repeal was eventually passed and the sev-
enteen Federalist courts were done away with. Nonetheless, in the
debate over the repeal of the law, the Republican side made it
clear that it was doing away with the Federalist judges and not
the independent authority of the courts.[30] After all, the Republicans now controlled the political branches of government; not
only could they appoint their own judges to the bench, they could
consider expanding the size of the Supreme Court to establish a
Republican majority at the highest level of the judiciary.[31] To
some degree, the judiciary was at the mercy of congressional
intent.

At the same time as the Federalist expansion of the judiciary
was being repealed, the courts were embroiled in another controversy. William Marbury was granted one of the judicial appointments made at the end of Adams's term. The appointment had
been approved by the Senate, signed by the president and given
over to the secretary of state, John Marshall, for delivery. Marshall himself left office to become a member of the Supreme
Court. When he left office, Marshall left to his brother James the
responsibility of delivering the completed judicial commissions to
Marbury and other last-minute appointees. The delivery was
never made, and when the Jefferson administration came into office, Secretary of State James Madison refused to deliver the completed judicial commissions that were pending. Marbury filed suit
in the Supreme Court, asking that pursuant to section 13 of the
Judiciary Act of 1789 the Court issue a writ of mandamus (a judicial order commanding the performance of a duty) ordering
Madison to deliver the commission.[32] Chief Justice Marshall was
now in a difficult position. The Federalist-packed judicial branch
was clearly under attack. For Marshall to order Madison to com-
ply with the law would set a dangerous precedent that probably
would not be complied with in any case. Therefore, Marshall set

a precedent, in his ruling in Marbury v. Madison (1803), that both expanded the power of the court and declined to intervene in the appointment of Marbury to the bench.

Marshall ruled that Marbury's legal rights had indeed been subverted, and he took that opportunity to scold the Jefferson administration concerning its faulty enforcement of the law. In the same decision, however, he declined to permit the Court to intervene. He ruled that section 13 of the Judiciary Act was unconstitutional in its delegation of authority to the courts. The Court could not constitutionally issue a writ of mandamus to require an executive official to act. Finally, Marshall took this opportunity to state the responsibility of the Court to rule on the constitutionality of the law:

> So if a law be in opposition to the constitution; if both the law and the constitution apply to a particular case, so that the court must either decide that case conformably to the law, disregarding the constitution; or conformably to the constitution, disregarding the law; the court must determine which of these conflicting rules governs the case. This is of the very essence of judicial duty.

> If, then, the courts are to regard the constitution, and the constitution is superior to any ordinary act of the legislature, the constitution, and not such ordinary act, must govern the case to which they both apply.[33]

Marshall's decision was a masterly political and technical performance. He had been sensitive to both the delicacies of the Court's current predicament and the inevitable direction of constitutional interpretation in regards to the powers of the Court. It was certain that Congress would pass laws that, in effect, would subvert the Constitution. If the Constitution was to have any meaning, the courts would have to have the power to pass judgment on the constitutionality of acts of Congress. Marbury v. Madison was inevitable from the moment that the framers decided to rely on structural mechanisms, the separation of powers, for the protection of individual liberties. In order for the courts to carry out their roles, they would have to be able to rule on the admissibility of the acts of the constituent parts of government.

Even after the ratification of the Eleventh Amendment, the repeal of the 1801 Circuit Court Act, and the refusal of the Court
to intervene in the Marbury controversy, the Supreme Court still
was under attack. Two months after the Marbury decision, Justice Samuel Chase in a public speech claimed that because of Republican attacks on the judiciary, the Constitution was about to
"sink into mobocracy." So angry were the Republicans in Congress about this attack, that in March 1804 the House of Representatives voted to impeach Chase.[34] In the Senate, when the
impeachment of Chase was tried, the Republican ranks were
riven over the question of the theory of impeachment. Certainly,
many senators reasoned, the Constitution did not mean that impeachment could be used for partisan purposes. Consequently,
the articles of impeachment against Justice Chase were overwhelmingly voted down; one was even voted down unanimously.
In the opinion of the Senate, to impeach Chase for what he had
said would forever compromise the independence of the judiciary.

The powers of the Court survived the controversial years of the
Jefferson administration. However, so chastened were the courts
by this experience, that the Supreme Court did not declare another act of Congress unconstitutional until fifty years later.[35] In
the 1857 Dred Scott decision, the court recognized the constitutionality of slavery and, at the same time, invalidated an act of
Congress that prohibited slavery north of the Mason-Dixon line.[36]
The distinguishing characteristic (from the legal standpoint) of
that decision was that the Court struck down a law that had
nothing to do with the judiciary. Concurrently, the Court sanctioned in its findings on the legality of slavery an extremely ambiguous interpretation of the Constitution. This was a departure
even from what Justice Marshall had tried to do in Marbury v.
Madison. With the Dred Scott decision, a decision that involved
an extremely broad exercise of judicial prerogative, the Supreme
Court began to take on the role we are so familiar with today.

The power of judicial review is not without limits, although
the extent of courts' power is difficult to trace. The task of interpreting the Constitution within a dynamic political environment

is not an exact science. The courts are constantly exploring new areas of constitutional interpretation as the context within which society operates continues to change. In addition, the courts respond to public opinion and political pressure. As the case of the politics of the Court under the Jeffersonians demonstrated, Congress, when it is so moved, does have the means to limit the decisions of the Court. Besides, the courts have neither an enforcement capability or an independent capacity to bring ongoing controversies to trial. The courts, therefore, must continuously walk a tightrope. To go beyond the limits of the acceptable in their interpretation of the law is to risk a political or public backlash—or simply to be ignored.

The public applies pressure on the courts in several ways. First, the electoral process may produce representatives in the political branches who profoundly affect the composition of the courts. President Reagan, in the eight years he was in office, made 360 life appointments to the federal bench, including 48 percent of the judges at the appellate level, 49 percent of the judges at the district level, and three Supreme Court justices. Legal experts agree that it is virtually impossible to bring to trial and win certain types of suits in the federal courts in the 1980s that would have been easily contestable in the 1970s.[37] In addition, appointments to the Supreme Court are more actively screened and are more than twice as likely to be rejected by the Senate than are appointments to the president's cabinet.[38] Second, while a relatively infrequent occurrence, constitutional amendments can be passed to circumvent existing court rulings. The Eleventh Amendment was not the only example of this. The Thirteenth, Fourteenth, and Fifteenth Amendments were ratified as a direct response to the Dred Scott decision. The Sixteenth Amendment, permitting the federal government to impose a direct income tax, was ratified to counteract a court ruling that overturned a tax law passed by Congress in 1894.[39] The Twenty-Sixth Amendment nullified a court decision to the effect that Congress was without power to set the voting age in state elections.[40] Third, Congress can pressure the courts through its constitutional power over the jurisdiction and composition of the courts.[41] Besides the Jeffersonian-era manipulations, Franklin Delano Roosevelt's "court-packing" scheme is the most famous modern example of a political branch attempting to use the legislative process (albeit unsuccessfully) to threaten and, perhaps, change the composition of the courts. Congress also has wide-ranging control over the jurisdiction and procedures of the courts.[42] The McCardle case is the classic example of the exercise of Congress's power over the jurisdiction of the courts.

In 1868 a newspaper editor from Mississippi (McCardle) who had been imprisoned by military occupying forces for publishing "incendiary and libelous articles" sued in the federal courts for a writ of habeas corpus. Congress had passed a law in February 1867 that authorized federal courts to grant habeas corpus to anyone held in violation of his constitutional rights. While this law was obviously intended to redress the abuses of liberty that occurred under slavery and as a result of the Civil War, McCardle attempted to apply a broader interpretation. At first, the courts ruled that they had jurisdiction over the matter.[43] The reconstruction Congress, however, not wanting to interfere with the authority of the military occupation of the South, passed a law in March 1868 that repealed the portion of the 1867 law giving the courts jurisdiction over the case.[44] The Supreme Court had no choice but to refuse the petitioner's request inasmuch as the Court no longer had jurisdiction.[45]

The McCardle case established a precedent for many years to follow. Congress often reacts to controversial decisions of the courts by attempting to adjust the courts' jurisdiction. While some of these laws have been challenged,[46] Congress has been generally successful in molding the courts' jurisdiction to serve political ends. Congressional control over federal court jurisdiction may take one of two forms.[47] First, Congress may control the progression through which federal cases proceed. For example, under the Voting Rights Act of 1965, a state seeking judicial review of a decision by the attorney general of the United States (to suspend the state's voting regulations) may apply for a hearing to the district court for the District of Columbia only.[48] Second, Congress may alter jurisdiction by creating special non-Article 3 legislative courts through which to channel certain issues. These courts do not operate under the tenure and justiciability requirements of Article 3. For example, under the Emergency Price Control Act of 1942, Congress established a special emergency court of appeals before which administrative action taken pursuant to the act could be reviewed. Military courts are also governed under a special set of procedures over which the federal courts have limited jurisdiction.[49]

In 1982 the Supreme Court responded to the challenges posed to the judicial prerogative by the establishment of Article 3 legislative courts. The Bankruptcy Act of 1978 established a special bankruptcy court in each judicial district. Pursuant to the act, bankruptcy judges on these courts were to serve fourteen-year terms and were to be paid salaries set by statute and subject to adjustment.[50] In the case of Northern Pipeline Construction Company v. Marathon Pipe Line Company, the court ruled the Bankruptcy Act's establishment of Article 3 legislative courts in this instance to be unconstitutional.[51] Justice Brennan, in his decision, concluded that because there were only special situations in which Article 3 courts could be created and because bankruptcy claims did not fit these criteria, Congress acted improperly in establishing these bankruptcy courts.[52] Furthermore, Brennan concluded that the establishment of Article 3 courts in this case constituted a threat to the independence and jurisdiction of the courts.[53]

Legislative and electoral sanctions are not the only way the public indirectly influences court decisions. While lobbying per se is not permitted in the courts, judges make reference to literature in their decisions other than the arguments presented by parties to the case in court. Law review articles, social science journals, briefs prepared by friends of the court (amicus curiae), and recent books are read by the judges and sometimes cited in their findings.

In addition, the courts must be conscious of their lack of enforcement powers. Noncompliance is always a possible outcome of the issuance of wide-ranging, unpopular, or impractical decisions. Perhaps the classic case of noncompliance came in the aftermath of the Chadha decision, in which the courts invalidated the legislative veto. As noted above, literally hundreds of legislative vetoes, both in statute and in informal understandings between the legislative and administrative branches, continue to be adopted and remain in force.[54] Prayers are still read in public schools all over the country despite the Court's decision banning state-sponsored prayer.[55] Southerners resisted for many years the Court's findings in Brown v. Board of Education;[56] the National Guard, pursuant to the president's command, eventually had to enforce the Court's rulings. Justice Holmes once said there was "no use talking about a law that will not be willingly obeyed by at least 90 percent of the population."[57] Justice Holmes's warning is aptly directed at the courts.

Charles Evans Hughes is often quoted as having said that "the Constitution is what the judges say it is." This, however, was an overstatement. The Constitution may be interpreted by the courts, but the law is the product of popular demand and the machinations of the political branches. There are a number of ways in which court rulings can be influenced or overturned. The courts are constantly at risk of being attacked as unresponsive, unaccountable, and out of the mainstream of American thought. Consequently, judges must take certain precautions in seeing that their edicts are enforced and that the legitimacy of the courts is maintained.[58]

In order to avoid conflicts with the political branches of government that would appear to subvert the notion of popular control over the government, the courts attempt to apply certain "cautionary considerations" in governing their power of judicial review.[59] Thus, while the outcomes of court decisions may have political repercussions, the process through which the courts arrive at their conclusions must be viewed as apolitical. For example, one cautionary rule is the requirement that courts not be permitted to issue "advisory opinions." An advisory opinion is a formal opinion expressed by a judge, but not as part of a lawsuit. In other countries (Great Britain, Canada, and Australia), advisory opinions are issued at the request of public officials. In the United States, however, the Supreme Court is barred from issuing advisory opinions because such a practice would be seen to prejudice the courts in advance of lawsuit filings and to intrude upon the responsibilities of the political branches.[60] The attorney general and the solicitor general are the government's lawyers, not the Court. Therefore, the attorney general will issue advisory opinions while the courts maintain a position of neutrality until a controversy is brought to trial. In their decisions, the justices have been known to hint at legislative remedies. However, the rule against issuing advisory opinions by the courts is rather strictly applied.[61]

The most important cautionary rule applied in defining the limits of the Court's prerogative is the doctrine of "political questions." The nomenclature of political questions confuses the issue. To suggest that the Court only rules on nonpolitical questions is oxymoronic. In fact, cases involving political questions are the most sensitive with which the Court has to deal. By choosing not to adjudicate such questions, the Court avoids some of its most dangerous (for the courts) forays into states' rights, presidential, and congressional powers. In order to maintain this doctrine, the Court has adopted some rather tortured reasoning. Perhaps the clearest statement of guidelines for the consideration of political questions occurs in Justice Brennan's opinion for the majority in the case of Baker v. Carr (1962). In breaking with tradition, the Supreme Court in that case decided to intervene in a state-level redistricting dispute that had been denied justiciability as a political question in a lower court.[62] The Supreme Court overruled the lower court, with Justice Brennan arguing that a nonjusticiable political question existed if there was:

1. a textually demonstrable constitutional commitment of the issue to a coordinate political department,

2. a lack of judicially discoverable and manageable standards for resolving the issue,

3. an impossibility of deciding without an initial policy determination,

4. an impossibility of deciding without undertaking an independent resolution that intrudes on the authority of coordinate branches of government,

5. an unusual need for adherence to a political decision already made,

6. potential embarrassment for multifarious pronouncements by various departments on one question.

This standard is, of course, ambiguous. If the Court is to make a judgment on the first requirement, it must, by implication, make a ruling on the issue. The doctrine of political questions in reality permits the Court to sidestep issues that would threaten the Court's legitimacy, status, and jurisdiction were the Court to intervene.

The Court must also exercise caution that its judgments not be seen as exercises of legislative power. There are two ways in which the Court can avoid the charge of legislative usurpation. The doctrine of *stare decisis* (stand by the precedents) dictates that the Court, whenever possible, abide by the past rulings of previous courts. In theory, as long as the Court is faithful to the principle of *stare decisis,* the Court maintains its legitimacy by becoming a link in a chain of decisions that connects it to the original Constitution. To deviate from the principle, would be to rob the Court of its links to the past. There are, of course, changes in conditions and factual errors made by previous courts that force the justices to overturn previous decisions. Nonetheless, *stare decisis* is fairly faithfully observed by the Court in its decisions.[63]

In addition, the courts generally attempt to adhere to a doctrine of "narrowness." In other words, the Court works to resolve disputes between parties to a lawsuit rather than invalidate the acts of Congress or of the states. Thus, it is not entirely accurate to say that the courts declare acts of the coordinate branches unconstitutional. The doctrine of judicial review is based on two assumptions. First, the Constitution operates of its own force. The Court simply recognizes constitutional principles that operate in contradiction of existing statutes. Statutes under review, if found unconstitutional, were never valid inasmuch as they violated the superior force of the Constitution. Second, the courts only rule on the dispute that involve the parties to the lawsuit. The Court does not invalidate a statute found unconstitutional. The Court only establishes the constitutional and overriding rule in a particular case.[64] Therefore, as long as the Court can appear to rule only on the narrow issues of the case, the Court can avoid the charge of interfering with the legislative function.[65]

Within the intrinsic limitations of the judicial function and constitutional role played by the Supreme Court, there is a certain amount of leeway the Court can exercise in trying cases. There are, to be sure, a number of "threshold requirements" that must be satisfied in order for the courts to accept a case for trial,[66] and these threshold requirements constitute yet another check on the courts. There is, however, a significant amount of dispute about the proper application of these threshold requirements. Therefore, these requirements may not be uniformly applied by the courts; neither do they constitute an absolute boundary on the judicial process.

In order that a case be justiciable, a case or controversy must meet several requirements.[67] First, cases must contain an adversarial controversy. The litigants to a dispute must disagree as to their interests or the case does not meet the standard of "adverseness." Second, the litigants in a case must establish "standing." The Court will only hear cases in which the plaintiffs can demonstrate that they have suffered some sort of injury that is the direct result of the actions of another party. For example in the case of Goldwater v. Carter, the Court refused to grant standing to sue to Senator Goldwater who was attempting to challenge President Carter's abrogation of a treaty existing between the United States and Taiwan. In the Court's opinion, Goldwater had no standing because the Senate had never taken a vote on the matter and Goldwater's voting rights as a Senator had not been breached.[68] Third, parties to a case must demonstrate that a controversy is "ripe" for adjudication or alternately not "moot." A case is thought to be ripe for adjudication if all administrative and legislative remedies have been exhausted. Again, Goldwater v. Carter is a good example of a case that was not ripe for adjudication. A case is thought to be moot if the controversy that brought the case to trial is no longer at issue. For example, when the states failed to ratify the Equal Rights Amendment, lawsuits challenging the extension by Congress of the period for ratification of the ERA were "mooted."[69]

The prerogative of judicial review is, then, both broad and limited. Judicial review is an important prerogative to the extent that the courts have established the tradition of ruling on the constitutionality of issues about which the framers never dreamed.[70] Nevertheless, the Court's power of judicial review operates under such severe restraints that we must regard Montesquieu's suggestion that the judicial branch "in a sense, has no force" as prescient.[71] While Montesquieu's claim may be overstated, the Court's decisions do lend tremendous force to the argument that the courts constitute "the least dangerous" branch of government.[72]

Finally, in order to carry out their responsibilities for adjudicating disputes, the courts have generated for themselves several prerogative powers that assist the courts in their assured provision of a "fair trial." Much like the congressional subpoena power and the associated enforcement mechanism of a contempt of Congress citation, the courts reserve for themselves the right to hold litigants, witnesses, petitioners, and observers in "contempt" for interfering with the judicial process. The courts have ruled in a number of cases that any behavior that prevents the administration of a fair trial is punishable as "contempt of court." In the case of Wood v. Georgia, the Court ruled, "we start with the premise that the right of courts to conduct their business in an untrammeled way lies at the foundation of our system of government."[73] One of the standards the Court uses in issuing contempt citations is the test of a "clear and present" danger to the judicial process.[74] In the case of Bridges v. California, the Supreme Court overturned a contempt citation that had been issued by California court when Harry Bridges, a union organizer, released to the public a telegram he had sent to the secretary of labor that predicted a massive strike if the California state court attempted to enforce its decision in a labor dispute. Justice Black held for the majority that the release of the telegram did not present a clear and present danger to the administration of justice.[75] This and other precedents indicate that almost anything said outside the courtroom is not punishable as contempt.[76] Judges are assumed to be resistant to outside pressure.[77]

Within the courtroom, however, the Court is much more willing to enforce its control. For example, in the case of Walker v. City of Birmingham, without considering the defendants' reasons for disobeying a court order, the Court found those who violated a court injunction (prohibiting parades without a permit) to be in contempt. Justice Stewart wrote in his decision, "respect for the judicial process is a small price to pay for the civilizing hand of law."[78] Defendants could violate a court injunction only if they could demonstrate that the Court did not possess the jurisdictional power to issue such an injunction or that the injunction ordered constituted an unconstitutional exercise of prior restraint.[79] The Court came to this conclusion despite the fact that the rules under which parade permits were required were subsequently found unconstitutional.[80]

One of the problems the courts face in providing a fair trial is ensuring that a defendant receive a trial free of bias generated by the outside publicity. On this issue the constitutional rights of a defendant are in conflict with the press's First Amendment protection against prior restraint.[81] In 1976 the Supreme Court reviewed a court order prohibiting the press from reporting news prejudicial to the defendant in a murder trial. The Supreme Court unanimously struck down the press restriction, with the majority of the Court arguing that the ban on press coverage "was of necessity speculative, dealing . . . with factors unknown and unknowable."[82] Consequently, by and large, the courts are reluctant to restrict public access to judicial proceedings (pursuant to the

Sixth Amendment guarantee of a "public trial"). Nevertheless, the courts have occasionally closed judicial proceedings (and, therefore, abridged First and probably Sixth Amendment rights) in order to protect victims in rape cases,[83] and to protect the identity of an undercover agent.[84]

The prerogative of the Court was born of a discarded doctrine of English constitutional law. The framers were unwilling to include the power of judicial review explicitly in the Constitution. When the Court did attempt to exercise this power, it was almost immediately under attack. The power of judicial review, unlike the expanded war power or the president's expanded authority under the commander in chief or chief executive clause, rests on extremely shaky political foundations. Inasmuch as judges are not elected and are appointed for life, the Court can easily be perceived as an undemocratic institution. To the extent that the power of judicial review is almost entirely a product of judicial construction, the constitutionality of the Court's adjudicatory authority is almost always subject to question. Because Congress and the president exercise control over the composition and jurisdiction of the courts, the judiciary is constantly at risk of being shaped and molded by political currents. The power of judicial review is, therefore, very carefully exercised.

Among the cautionary restraints the courts have adopted are the principle of *stare decisis* and the doctrine of political questions. To be safe, the courts avoid any action that could be construed to be an usurpation of the power of the coordinate branches of government. Cases are, for the most part, carefully decided within the bounds of previously accepted precedents. In general, the courts choose not to rule beyond the specific facts of the dispute, and many controversial disputes are simply judged nonjusticiable. The power of judicial review is, as the term "construction" implies, a glacial force. Judicial adjustments to the law come slowly. There have been activist courts that go beyond the limits of cautionary restraints; these activists, however, are the exception rather than the rule, and they proceed at their own risk.

There are also intrinsic limitations to the judicial process itself. The Court cannot on its authority bring trial lawsuits over controversial issues. It must wait for the proper filing of well-suited test cases. The Court lacks the power to enforce its own decisions. Many unpopular decisions are simply ignored. This, in itself, acts as a constraint on the Court's ability to issue far-reaching rulings. The legitimacy of the Court's authority is eroded when the decisions of the Court are not enforced.

The prerogative of the Court should not be exaggerated. The activism of the Warren Court or fear of the consequences of the Reagan appointees should not be overstated. There is always a political remedy to a recalcitrant judiciary. Congress and the president are fully capable of reversing or at least influencing trends in judicial construction. One suspects, then, that the judiciary acts as a kind of lightning rod for criticism as it steers the Constitution through inevitable and necessary, albeit unpopular, changes. In that sense, the myth of judicial supremacy serves the interests of the representatives in the political branches. The courts are forced to make final and definitive judgments concerning controversial issues. Politicians then have the luxury of escaping responsibility for unpopular decisions made by the courts.

6 Prerogative Powers and the Constitution

There is no question that the federal government exercises powers as potentially far-reaching as the power of medieval kings. The difference is that in the United States, under the rule of law, prerogative powers are generally not exercised arbitrarily. There have been cases in which the extraordinary powers of government have been abused, but to overemphasize this abuse is to beg the question of whether or not the regular exercise of prerogative powers is constitutional. Does the Constitution as it is written contain the grants of power necessary for its own protection? The Constitution does include open-ended clauses that may provide for the exercise of extraordinary powers. However, whether these "elastic clauses" were intended to justify the occasional violation of personal liberties is questionable. It is more likely that because any set of structures and laws, particularly in a constitution that is more than two hundred years old, are bound to be somewhat dated and because the written word can never completely capture the aspirations of a society, we have to be prepared to discuss a different notion of constitutionalism: an expansive constitutionalism that serves the needs of modern society while maintaining important links to the past.

Is there any reason to believe that the justification for the exercise of prerogative powers can be gleaned from the text of the Constitution itself? There are, in fact, open-ended grants of power in the Constitution under which the prerogative powers of government may be subsumed. For example, a likely vehicle for an interpretive justification of extraordinary powers is the so-called necessary and proper clause. A study of the historical development of government policy based on this particular clause, however, demonstrates some of the limitations and contradictions of the contention that the Constitution contains within itself the resources necessary for its own protection.

Article 1, section 8 reads "The Congress shall have power . . . To make all laws which shall be necessary and proper for carrying into execution the foregoing powers, and all other powers vested by this Constitution in the government of the United States, or in any department or officer thereof." One of the earliest controversies concerning the meaning of the necessary and proper clause took place in 1790, when Congress passed a bill authorizing the establishment of a Bank of the United States. Secretary of the Treasury Alexander Hamilton had urged the incorporation of a national bank in order to facilitate interstate commerce and the collection of federal taxes. Washington was not altogether certain that Congress had the power under the Constitution to establish such a bank. He requested advisory opinions on the matter from both his secretary of state, Thomas Jefferson, and his secretary of treasury. This rather heated exchange was representative of the ongoing struggle over the meaning of the Constitution in regards to the limits of the powers of the federal government.[1]

Jefferson argued that the establishment of the Bank was not permissible, inasmuch as "all powers not delegated to the United States, by the Constitution, not prohibited by it to the States, are reserved to the States or to the people."[2] The creation of the Bank, therefore, was unconstitutional to the extent that there was no *specific* grant in the Constitution authorizing the establishment of such a bank. Also, he argued, the *general* provisions of the Constitution such as the necessary and proper clause could not be construed to authorize such an action. Jefferson's reasoning rested on his interpretation of the word "necessary" as it was used in Article I, section 9. Jefferson believed that the necessary and proper clause authorized nothing more than actions that were absolutely essential for carrying out the specifically enumerated grants of power under the Constitution. Inasmuch as the

Bank of the United States was merely a convenience, the necessary and proper clause could not be used as a justification for going beyond the written constitution.[3]

Hamilton vehemently disagreed. He believed that the creation of government corporations was an ancillary power associated with the sovereignty of the United States. To the extent that the United States had the power to collect taxes or to regulate interstate commerce, he argued, the power to create corporations to serve those ends were implied powers. But the implied powers of the federal government extended only to the limits of the sovereignty of the United States. For example, the federal government had no authority to police the city of Philadelphia (his example). Thus, the federal government could not establish a corporation responsible for policing that city. In addition, Hamilton found Jefferson's interpretation of the word "necessary" to be particularly absurd. "To understand the word [necessary] as the Secretary of State does," Hamilton wrote, "would be to depart from its obvious and popular sense, and to give it a restrictive operation, an idea never before entertained. It would be to give it the same force as if the word *absolutely* or *indispensably* had been prefixed to it." Hamilton went on to argue:

This restrictive interpretation of the word *necessary* is also contrary to this sound maxim of construction: Namely, that the powers contained in a constitution of government, especially those which concern the general administration of the affairs of a country, its finances, trade, defence, etc., ought to be construed liberally in advancement of the public good. . . . The means by which national exigencies are to be provided for, national inconveniences obviated, national prosperity promoted, are of such infinite variety, extent, and complexity, that there must of necessity be great latitude of discretion in the selection and application of those means.[4]

Washington signed the Bank bill. However, Hamilton's expansive view of the government's powers were not accepted in their totality by the other great leaders of his time.[5]

Washington seemed to accept a fairly broad definition of the necessary and proper clause. In his last message to Congress, he proposed a series of measures that would have almost certainly been rejected under Jefferson's interpretation of the Constitution. In his final message he stated:

Congress have repeatedly, and not without success, directed their attention to the encouragement of manufactures. The object is of too much consequence not to insure a continuance of their efforts in every way which shall appear eligible. As a general rule, manufactures on public account are inexpedient: but where the state of things in a country leaves little hope that certain branches of manufacture will for a great length of time obtain, when these are of a nature essential to the furnishing and equipping of the public force in time of war, are not establishments for procuring them on public account to the extent of the ordinary demand for the public service recommended by strong considerations of national policy as an exception to the general rule?[6]

More than anything else, Washington seemed concerned about the efficacy of government interference in the market. However, when in the course of public policy making, government interference contributed to the public good, Washington was not reluctant to encourage an activist public policy.

It seems somewhat quaint now to recall an era when presidents were reluctant to approve the construction of public works by the federal government. However, because it was never clear how much the imposition of public works financed by the federal government intruded upon the rights of states, there were some who believed in the early days of the republic that federal expenditures for public works were unconstitutional. Not the least of the illustrious opponents of this type of public expenditure was James Madison. In 1817, Congress passed a bill appropriating funds for the building of national roads and canals. Madison vetoed the bill, arguing:

The legislative powers vested in Congress are specified and enumerated in the 8th section of the first article of the Constitution; and it does not appear that the power proposed to be exercised by the bill is among the enumerated powers; or that it falls, by any just interpretation, within the power to make laws necessary and proper for carrying into execution those or other powers vested by the Constitution in the Government of the United States.[7]

In 1822, James Monroe vetoed a public works bill for the same general reasons and suggested that the Constitution be amended to allow for the funding of public works by the federal government.[8] Such an amendment was never adopted; yet, in the modern era billions of dollars are spent by the federal government for the purpose of public works. The necessary and proper clause has obviously been broadly reinterpreted. But has it been sufficiently broadened to allow for the constitutional exercise of prerogative powers as documented in the previous chapters?

A number of factors contributed to this shift in the perceived legitimacy of an activist national government. In general, federal regulation and participation in the interstate economy became increasingly important in the first half of the nineteenth century. More specifically, the political atmosphere changed. In 1825, John Quincy Adams, a strong supporter of an activist role for the federal government, was elected to the presidency. He immediately proposed a broad program of federal expenditures intended to facilitate transportation and education at the national level. His position was bolstered by two important court decisions, McCulloch v. Maryland (1819) and Gibbons v. Ogden (1824). In his decision in McCulloch v. Maryland, Justice John Marshall made it clear that the necessary and proper clause did not stand in the way of the exercise and supremacy of federal powers. The Hamiltonian interpretation held sway, but the outer limits of those "necessary" powers were still to be decided.[9] In Gibbons v. Ogden, the Supreme Court overturned a New York State statute designed to regulate steamboat traffic on the Hudson River.[10] These cases, the "nullification crisis," and, ultimately, the Civil War indisputably established the supremacy of the federal government.

In 1816, James Madison signed legislation that chartered a second Bank of the United States.[11] The state of Maryland imposed a state tax on the operations of the Baltimore branch of that Bank. James McCulloch, cashier of the federal bank, refused to pay and was sued by the state of Maryland for collection of those taxes. McCulloch countersued, arguing that the Maryland law was unconstitutional. The state court of Maryland ruled in favor of the state and McCulloch appealed the case to the federal courts. In his Supreme Court decision, Justice Marshall rejected the state's claim that the exclusive sovereignty of the states precluded the establishment of a national bank. He also rejected the state's claim that the necessary and proper clause prevented Congress from chartering a national bank. On this point, Marshall's argument, as well as the argument made by the state of Maryland respectively mirror the assertions made on the same issues by Jefferson and Hamilton twenty-eight years earlier. The controversy surrounding the issue of state sovereignty again primarily rested on the meaning of the word "necessary." Justice Marshall dismissed the state of Maryland's contention that the word necessary, as it was used in Article 1, section 8 of the Constitution was intended to mean *absolutely* necessary. Instead, he argued that the meaning of words had to be divined from "the subject, the context, [and] the intention of the person using them. Let this be done in the case under consideration." He continued:

The subject is the execution of those great powers on which the welfare of a nation essentially depends. It must have been the intention of those who gave these powers, to insure, as far as human prudence could insure, their beneficial execution. This could not be done by confiding the choice of means to such narrow limits as not to leave it in the power of Congress to adopt any which might be appropriate, and which were conducive to the end. This provision is made in a constitution intended to endure for ages to come, and, consequently, to be adapted to the various crises of human affairs.[12]

This statement, taken out of context, might be misconstrued to mean that the necessary and proper clause validates the exercise of almost any power by the federal government. Even so, a textual review of Justice Marshall's decision reveals that he was fully prepared to find in favor of McCulloch on the basis of the other enumerated powers of Congress under Article 1, section 8.[13] In other words, the expanded interpretation of the necessary and proper clause was not essential to establish the supremacy of the federal government in this case. Furthermore, Justice Marshall, in discussing the meaning of the necessary and proper clause, implied that the means necessary for the pursuit of government ends are only permissible insofar as they are not prohibited by other parts of the Constitution.[14] Congress cannot use the necessary and proper clause to authorize actions that violate other portions of the Constitution.[15] The necessary and proper clause, therefore, does not justify the exercise of prerogative powers that violate the Bill of Rights.

The courts have since reaffirmed this rather generous, Hamiltonian reading of the necessary and proper clause and also clarified its restrictions as well. In Reid v. Covert (1957), the Court ruled that military law could not be extended to include civilians in peacetime. In the case of a crime committed by a military dependent on a military base, the government argued that the necessary and proper clause justified the extension of military justice to dependents living on military posts. The Court rejected this claim, arguing that the necessary and proper clause could not be used as an excuse to suspend the Bill of Rights, even for military dependents. The Court later reaffirmed this interpretation in Kinsella v. Singleton (1980). In that case Justice Clark, writing for the majority, suggested that the necessary and proper clause itself is not a grant of power, "but a caveat that the Congress possesses all the means necessary to carry out the specifically granted 'foregoing' powers."[16]

What this exploration of the necessary and proper clause illustrates is that trying to develop a textual exegesis based on case law that justifies the exercise of prerogative powers is extremely difficult. The Constitution contains its own internal contradictions that on the one hand supply the government with the means for its own protection, but on the other hand limit those means. This is a paradox of constitutionalism in a democracy. A constitutional democracy is in some ways a contradiction in terms. As noted constitutional scholar Charles Howard McIlwain once put it:

Constitutionalism suffers from the defects inherent in its own merits. Because it cannot do some evil it is precluded from doing some good. Shall we, then forego the good to prevent the evil, or shall we submit to the evil to secure the good? This is the fundamental practical question of all constitutionalism.[17]

A constitution is a structure through which a democracy restricts its own actions according to some previously agreed-to set of principles.[18] In that sense, a constitution will inevitably be at some times and in some ways antidemocratic. The primary task, then, in justifying an action of government according to the Constitution is identifying whether or not that action conforms to the government's constituent principles. There is no question that prerogative powers are sometimes antidemocratic.[19] The problem to be solved then becomes whether there is any overriding constitutional justification for the exercise of extraordinary powers even when those powers violate the liberties guaranteed by the Bill of Rights.

Clinton Rossiter once suggested that the Constitution is "equal to any emergency."[20] His assertion has not been universally accepted. Certainly, the government can and has exercised a broad range of extraordinary powers, sometimes in situations that can only loosely be termed emergencies. Whether these actions constitute exercises of governmental powers within the meaning of the Constitution, however, is another question. By what standards are we willing to evaluate the constitutionality of the exercise of prerogative powers?

According to one standard, it is still possible to view the Constitution from the Lockean perspective. Locke argued that it was sometimes necessary for a government to act, "for the public good, without the prescription of the law."[21] Presumably, then, the exercise of prerogative powers according to this view is necessary but unconstitutional. Consequently, the Constitution is *not* equal to any emergency. For example, legal scholar Sotirios Barber argues that government leaders occasionally take actions, of necessity, that do not conform to the Constitution. This is not to say that these actions are improper, he argues. Rather, this is to say that these actions can in no way be construed as constitutional.[22] For instance, Barber cites the example of Abraham

Lincoln who suspended the writ of habeas corpus in some regions
at the beginning of the Civil War. Under Article 1, section 9 of
the Constitution, the writ may be suspended in "cases of rebellion." It is not clear from reading the constitutional text with
whom the power to suspend the writ resides. Nonetheless, Lincoln ordered his suspensions at the beginning of the revolt before
Congress came into session.

On 4 July 1861 President Lincoln defended his actions to Congress:

These measures, whether strictly legal or not, were ventured upon, under what appeared to be a popular demand, and a public necessity;
trusting, then as now, that Congress would readily ratify them. It is believed that nothing has been done beyond the constitutional competency
of Congress.[23]

Congress eventually voted a retroactive approval of the president's actions in August of that same year. Barber argues that inasmuch as the Constitution cannot be construed to allow the
president to suspend the writ of habeas corpus without the concurrence of Congress, Lincoln "as a person strategically posi-
tioned, not strictly as president, chose to violate the law."[24]
Lincoln was, then, according to Barber, exercising the "Lockean
prerogative" that *any* person may employ, in extraordinary situations, to justify revolution or "milder forms of disobedience on
the part of the president or anyone else."[25] The conflict in this
case, Barber insists, was "not between the rules of the Constitution," but "between the Constitution and events. The Constitution and the time do not always jibe."[26]

There are several problems with this argument. First, it is not
entirely clear that Lincoln's suspension of the writ was unconstitutional. The Court's majority ruling in the Prize Cases seems to
dispute this contention.[27] Consequently, assuming that the suspension controversy is the best example that Barber can produce,
it is not clear that there does not exist those "certain and unalterable laws" (Locke's terminology) by which a president can
constitutionally act without having to rely on prerogative powers.[28]
In fact, the state through the Constitution is liberally provided

with the means for self-defense and self-preservation. Further-more, Barber's interpretation of the concept of Lockean prerog-ative in this instance is questionable. Even though there is a strong connection in the American political tradition between the Lockean concept of natural rights and the belief that governments in violation of those natural rights lose their legitimacy,[29] it is not clear whether this Lockean principle of self-defense can be justi-fiably transferred to the president and other highly placed actors in the government.[30]

The most troubling aspect of Barber's analysis, however, is the lack of standards for determining the limits of the exercise of pre-rogative powers. I fear this kind of analysis simply because the Lockean prerogative is so open-ended. By reliance on this sort of standard of legality, by arguing that unconstitutional acts are "proper" if they are "necessary," we confront a tautological jus-tification for the exercise of prerogative powers. In effect, accord-ing to this analysis, there are no firm standards by which to judge the legality of extraordinary acts.

In contrast to Barber's contention that there is such a thing as an unconstitutional act appropriate to the salvation of the repub-lic, it can be argued that the Constitution is infinitely malleable. Arthur Miller, another noted legal scholar, argues that there is potentially no limit to constitutionality. The Constitution is what the rich and powerful say it is. The Constitution, Miller argues, is really two documents: the "political" constitution establishes the structure of government, and the "economic" constitution guarantees and protects the property of individuals.[31] As an eco-nomic document, Miller suggests, the Constitution acts to em-power an economic "elite" that uses the structure of government to its own advantage.[32] Political outcomes are dictated, therefore, by a ruling class in America, and any constitutional principle can be adjusted to fit the needs of the elite.[33]

Miller's argument is only the most extreme example of a genre in constitutional analysis that suggests that the Constitution is merely a shell within which political maneuvering takes place.[34] This genre is sometimes termed the *noninterpretivist* school of constitutional scholarship. Noninterpretivists believe that the "courts should . . . enforce norms that cannot be discovered within the four corners of the [Constitution]."[35] Interpretivists, by contrast, believe that judges in deciding constitutional issues should "confine themselves to enforcing norms that are stated."[36] Miller goes one step beyond the noninterpretivist construct to suggest that the outcome of the political struggle is controlled by a political elite. In doing so, Miller opens his analysis to a number of critiques.

First, there is ample evidence to suggest that "elite theory" is a post hoc, nonfalsifiable, misinterpretation of the fact that decision making in the United States is class-biased.[37] Elite theorists go one step further (unjustifiably, I would argue) to suggest that the class bias in decision making is reflective of elite "control." More importantly, noninterpretivist approaches are to be criticized as being inconsistent with the notion of constitutionalism. To suggest that a constitution can be open-ended is a contradiction in terms. Law, as such, cannot exist without objective standards for its enforcement and constitutions cannot exist without law.[38] A government that operates without the constraint of law is, in effect, an authoritarian regime. To suggest, as Miller does, that American constitutional law is merely a reflection of the structure of power in society is to falsely categorize the American government as authoritarian.

If, as Miller argues, its constitutional standards are simply a function of power relationships, the United States is essentially a lawless state. The "law" is whatever the rich and powerful deem it to be. To apply this analysis to the United States, however, is to lump the United States with other, lawless nations such as, for instance, Lebanon, in which power is the ultima ratio of disputes. Such a comparison is ridiculous. As Samuel Huntington argued in *Political Order in Changing Societies,* a more useful distinction to make between countries is the distinction that draws a line between "effective" and "debile" political systems. An effective political system, according to Huntington, "is a political community with an overwhelming consensus among the people on the legitimacy of the political system."[39] Clearly, the United States, according to this standard, is an "effective" state and Lebanon is not. Something beyond simple power of class in American society regulates the outcomes of constitutional disputes.

If the primary standard for the establishment of an effective state is the existence of some kind of national consensus, it may be possible to argue that an expanded notion of constitutionalism, one that relies on this requirement of consensus, can account for and supply standards for the appropriate exercise of extraordinary powers within the Constitution. A construct of this kind is presented by John Hart Ely, who argues "that the original Constitution, was principally, indeed I would say overwhelmingly, dedicated to concerns of process and structure and not to the identification and preservation of specific substantive values."[40] Consequently, he concludes, the primary responsibility of the courts in interpreting the Constitution is to preserve that structure.[41] In order to protect the structure of American constitutional government, preserving the "process of representation," or the intricate connection between the rulers and the ruled, is the most important goal of the courts.[42] As long as the representative process is preserved, he argues, we can assume "that an effective majority will not inordinately threaten its own rights, and . . . not systematically treat others less well than it treats itself."[43]

Ely's analysis is faithful to the notion of constitutionalism. There are many objective standards by which to judge the constitutionality of the political process. Therefore, we may regard rules that govern the political process as "law" in every sense of the term. For example, it is very hard to interpret as open-ended constitutional standards for the terms, qualifications, and procedures to be followed by our representatives in government. I refer again at this point to Justice Hughes's opinion in Home Building and Loan Association v. Blaisdell (1934) in which Hughes made the distinction between those constitutional provisions that were eligible for construction and those provisions that were not. The fact that two senators are to be elected from every state, for example, is very difficult to construe in any other way except for its exact meaning.

Where Ely's analysis falls afoul of the notion of constitutionalism is in the application of his principles to exceptional cases, that is, instances in which the representative process cannot be made to work. In exceptional cases such as in the early days of the Civil War or World War II, the representative process, as a whole, either breaks down or is absent. We are then forced to rely on the prospect that our representatives (those who are in a position to act) will, as Thomas Jefferson argued, do as we would have done.[44] But are there any limits, implicit or explicit, to these exercises of prerogative powers in emergencies? Neither Barber nor Ely (nor Miller, for that matter) deal successfully with this problem.

The fact is, in the United States the rule of law seems not to break down, even in the most dire situations. It is interesting to note that even in the most desperate moments of American history, national elections were held (1864 and 1944) and that the coordinate branches continued to operate in these contexts, sometimes even in opposition to the president's plans.[45] While Franklin Delano Roosevelt threatened to carry out his plans whether or not his actions were approved by Congress, these threats were never put to the test.[46] Yet we can clearly remember instances in which presidents were accused of and eventually restrained from committing unconstitutional acts. For example, Richard Nixon was ordered by the courts to release funds impounded for policy purposes and to release tapes withheld for the purpose of stymieing congressional investigations. Standards do seem to exist governing the use of power in extraordinary situations, but what are the principles that maintain the rule of law in emergencies?

What seems to have protected the American Constitution in times of emergency is an overwhelming consensus that overlays the law and, yet, protects the Constitution. An "effective" constitution, therefore, is one that comprises *both* law and consensus.[47] If constitutions were simply structures of law, any constitution would be the equal of the American Constitution. Yet, within the United States, within Britain, and within other "constitutional" regimes there is a measure of cooperation on the part of citizens and adherence to the law on the part of the government that transcends coercion.[48] For example, while there are high levels of tax evasion in the United States, what is more remarkable is the level of compliance. The tax system in the United States would collapse, as it has in many less-developed states, without extraordinarily high levels of voluntary cooperation. The cooperation without coercion of citizens in a society must be evidence of the existence of contractual component to constitutionalism. Constitutions are both a construct of law and a construct of principles. The contractual principles underlying the law in a constitution, are the foundation upon which the rule of law stands. When the rule of law is short-circuited, as it is in an emergency, the principles that form the social contract are the ultimate resource for the protection of the constitution.

Having identified a standard beyond law for the measurement of constitutionalism, wherein lies the "consensus" of the American State? It is difficult to identify, as a practical matter, a consensus in American politics. Justice Story wrote:

Human nature never yet presented the extraordinary spectacle of all minds agreeing in all things; nay, not in all truths, moral, political, civil, or religious. . . . Did any statesman ever conceive the project of a constitution of government for a nation or State, every one of whose powers and operations should be liable to be suspended at the will of any one who should doubt their constitutionality?[49]

The framers, as a group, were never in complete agreement about the moral principles upon which this country was to be founded. Even the Declaration of Independence, which is reputed to be the primary American statement of natural rights, was, as we have seen, more of an indictment of the abuses specific to the rule of King George III. In fact, the colonists, for the most part, objected to the structural failings of British colonial rule. It should come as no surprise, therefore, that the Articles of Confederation and, later, the Constitution were primarily institutional arrangements.

Even later, the Bill of Rights met with acceptance, but not with universal approbation.[50]

Nevertheless, one unifying thread is an enduring faith in "due process." Not the due process as narrowly conceived of in the Fifth, Sixth, or Fourteenth Amendments, but the due process that is enshrined in the structures of the Constitution. The framers had a notion that the structure of politics could be regarded as and would operate as a science. Washington called for the establishment of a national university for the study of politics as a science.[51] Jefferson likened the structure of the Constitution to "the plants revolving round their common sun, acting and acted upon according to their respective weights and distances." The Constitution, Jefferson believed, "will produce that beautiful equilibrium on which our Constitution is founded, and which I believe it will exhibit to the world in a degree of perfection, unexampled but in the planetary system itself."[52] Hamilton, in defending the outlines of the new federalist system wrote:

The science of politics . . . like most other sciences, has received great improvement. The efficacy of various principles is now well understood, which were either not known at all, or imperfectly known to the ancients. The regular distribution of power into distinct departments; the introduction of legislative balances and checks; the institution of courts composed of judges holding their offices during good behavior; the representation of the people in the legislature by deputies of their own election; these are wholly new discoveries.[53]

These are but a few examples of the framers' profound belief in the existence in a science of politics. The belief in the science of politics is another unifying theme in American politics.[54] This "faith in science" as an underlying value in the constitution of the United States, manifests itself in both the *practice* and the *principle* of process. Not only is the Constitution designed to provide a set of structures, the undergirding principle that supports the Constitution in emergency or in unprecedented situations is a faith in the science of politics.

There are certain advantages to this focus on procedure and structure in the political system. The focus on procedure provides an objective standard for determining what is or is not the *law* and, ultimately, what is constitutional. This is not to say that the procedures or outcomes of the political process are value-neutral or are completely discoverable. In fact, it can be easily demonstrated that the legal and political system in the United States is somewhat class-biased.[55] The "consensus," such as it is in American politics, does not concern agreements over interpretations of the Bill of Rights or other notions of justice. There is, in fact, a wide disparity of beliefs concerning the meaning of freedom of speech, of the press, and so on. The only way to reconcile this disparity of beliefs peaceably is to interpose the government as an arbiter. There is no guarantee, however, to the participants in the political struggle that the government will be a completely unbiased arbiter. Neither is it true that just because the government may be biased, that its decisions are completely made at random or in the interest of a ruling elite.[56] There is an intermediate conclusion to be drawn about the limits of constitutional law.

Constitutional law can only exist to provide procedures and some general guidelines (moral and procedural) to be followed in every instance except emergencies. In respect to the prerogative powers, the process of government seems to be the key; that is, not the actual process itself, but the *principle* of process. The standard by which to measure the legitimacy of prerogative acts is whether, in the absence of the availability of the representative process, the principle of process has been adhered to. By and large, extraordinary actions taken in times of emergency have met with acceptance on the part of the coordinate branches of government. When the government as a whole is not able to convene in case of an emergency, most exercises of prerogative power by the president have been approved after the fact. There are, of course, honest disagreements as to the constitutionality of certain actions. However, there are certain claims to power that are not made and there have been, historically, exercises of power that have not been accepted. These instances in which the limits of constitutional law may have been breached are the markers of the limit of the law.

In peacetime, the prerogatives of government are delimited by the process of representation and by the principle of liberty protected under the Bill of Rights. In the exercise of their prerogative powers, the different branches of government are responsible to one another through checks and balances and responsible to the population through the structure of elections. In addition, under normal circumstances (i.e., in the absence of war or emergency) the freedoms guaranteed under the Bill of Rights may not be abridged (with a few, relatively minor exceptions).[57]

Congress, in exercising its primary prerogative, the oversight function, has the power to subpoena witnesses, hold noncompliant witnesses in contempt of Congress, require the testimony of executive branch officials, and require from the executive branch the submission of all materials relevant to a congressional investigation. Congress may not in its investigations inquire into matters not related to legislation, the private affairs of individuals, or certain "privileged" communications within the executive branch. In order to facilitate the exercise of this oversight prerogative Congress has developed for itself several tools, including increased staffing and budgets, independent congressional investigatory and research agencies, congressional participation in various treaty negotiations, delegations to international organizations and various advisory commissions, the legislative veto (and its functional equivalents), and reporting requirements.

The primary presidential prerogative in peacetime is associated with the president's power as chief executive. In order to administer the laws, the president and his agents must make decisions as to the meaning of congressional intent and the applicability of the law at a variety of stages of implementation. Interpretation of the law requires the issuance of written regulations that are now, since the late 1970s, subject to review by the OMB. The president may also impound appropriated funds pursuant to congressional approval. In diplomacy, the president may enter into executive agreements, the primary purpose of which is to execute existing treaties or statutes. The president is required by law to report to Congress the text of all executive agreements.[58] The president has also developed a number of tools to assist in the conduct of the administrative prerogative. The size and professionalism of the executive office of the president has been enhanced. In particular, the staff and budget of the OMB and the NSC have been augmented.

The primary prerogative of the courts in peacetime or in war is the power of judicial review. The courts may declare unconstitutional the acts of the states or the coordinate political branches of government. The courts are severely limited in their exercise of judicial review to the extent that they are unable to enforce their decisions and are only able to make a constitutional determination when an appropriate case is brought before them for adjudication. In addition, the courts are constantly at risk of being viewed as essentially undemocratic. Therefore, in the exercise of judicial review the courts have developed a set of principles to ensure that the judiciary will be viewed as a neutral actor. The limitations imposed by the principle of *stare decisis,* the doctrines of mootness, and standing, among others, protect the integrity of the courts. The president and Congress are fully capable of adjusting the courts' jurisdiction, composition, and even its decisions.

This brief review of the prerogative powers of the coordinate branches of government reveals a pattern. No prerogative in peacetime is exercised beyond the control of the other branches. There are relatively intelligible standards that serve to establish whether one branch or another has properly exercised its power. The proper exercise of prerogative power in peacetime, therefore, conforms rather closely to Ely's notion of the Constitution as a process of representation. Procedural guarantees are simply an extension of the representative structure of government. The problem with this analysis is that it is not all-encompassing, especially with regard to the exercise of prerogative powers in an emergency.

The president in wartime exercises a tremendous array of powers. I have documented in previous chapters a number of situations in which the president violated the rights of citizens in wartime. Civilians have been held for military trial, the writ of habeas corpus has been suspended, citizens have been forcibly moved from their homes, and all manner of freedoms "guaranteed" under the First Amendment have been violated. While these actions seem to be without limits there is a definite pattern in their exercise. Emergency actions taken in the absence of the concurrence of the coordinate branches are subject to definite time limits. As the court found in the Yakus case the existence of an "emergency" is a function of the context and not of the president's declaration of a state of emergency. Emergency actions taken without the concurrence of the coordinate branches can only be taken as long as it is physically impossible for the other branches to convene. The courts are very clear that congressional concurrence to, and authorization of, the wartime acts of the president is essential whenever possible. This does not mean that Congress *must* act. Rather, Congress must be informed and be given every opportunity to act. It must be assumed, then, that the absence of congressional action during a state of emergency (if Congress is in session) is an implied assent. For example, Congress must bear equal responsibility for the conduct of the Vietnam War, even after the repeal of the Gulf of Tonkin Resolution. Congress, however, is not responsible for the disastrous Iranian hostage-rescue mission, about which it was not adequately informed.[59]

The exercise of extraordinary powers must be proportionate to the risk. The president, and ultimately Congress, must demonstrate that there is some kind of connection between the action taken and the risks involved. As Justice Clark wrote in the Youngstown case, "the President's independent power to act depends upon the gravity of the situation confronting the nation."[60] There is, of course, no way to make a definitive judgment in this regard. What is a proportionate response to some would not be so to others. Rather, the objective standard by which proportionality must be measured is whether or not the coordinate branches have been informed and, whenever possible, allowed to act. Here, again, the coordinate branches should not be required to act in the affirmative. The existence of the *opportunity* to act must be considered tantamount to assent. The opportunity to act in assent only exists when Congress is fully informed and citizens injured by the prerogative actions of government are allowed to exhaust their grievances in the courts. We should fully expect that injured parties (and Congress) will claim their rights in a way and with a zeal that cannot be approximated by the establishment of artificial standards.[61]

The president, in particular, must be willing to abide by the decisions of the coordinate branches. The president must discontinue the exercise of an emergency prerogative if directly contravened by Congress together with the courts. This requirement, of course, is no guarantee that the president will obey the dictates of Congress in this regard. However, this principle sets a standard for the constitutional exercise of prerogatives.

The Supreme Court plays a special, albeit limited, role in the exercise of prerogative powers. Inasmuch as the Court is bound by precedent and the strict confines of the written constitution, it may not be institutionally well suited for serving as the forum of last resort in deciding the constitutionality of the exercises of prerogative. Situations that call for the exercise of prerogative powers, by definition, do not conform to precedent or written law. The Court, therefore, should have very little to say about the exercise of prerogative powers except to lend its considerable prestige to rulings concerning the proper procedures to be followed in the exercise of prerogatives. The Court can take advantage of the fact that there are discoverable standards by which to measure whether, in the exercise of emergency prerogatives, the president has conformed to the *principle* of process.

In applying these standards to Lincoln's suspension of habeas corpus, we must come to the conclusion that Lincoln acted constitutionally. Inasmuch as Congress was out of session at the beginning of the revolt, Lincoln was in the position to determine, on his own, the measures to be taken in response. While there are some disagreements as to whether Lincoln's actions between the beginning of the war and the time that Congress came into session were commensurate to the threat, Lincoln never claimed that his power was not subject to the review of the Congress and the courts. When, in one case, the Court challenged Lincoln's suspension of the writ, the prisoner in question was turned over to civilian authorities.[62] When Congress came back into session, Lincoln's action received limited but not complete congressional approval. While Lincoln may have intimated that he would continue to exercise his wartime prerogatives whether or not Congress approved, his defiance of Congress was never put to the test.[63] Therefore, we must come to the conclusion that in the early days of the Civil War the "spirit," if not the letter, of the Constitution was observed.

The *principle* of process then guides the exercise of prerogative in situations in which the process itself is disrupted. Is this constitutional? I would say it is. To expect the Constitution to guide decision making in all situations is impossibly naive. By the same token, to suggest that all actions taken by governmental officials in emergencies not traceable to constitutional text are simply actions taken outside the law, is more than a little dangerous. The Constitution as writ large was designed to guide the government in the normal course of policy making as well as in the breach. By what constitutional principles do we, then, guide the exercise of extraordinary powers? The strings that tie us to our founding past are the institutions the framers established. Institutions have lives that extend beyond human mortality. In that sense, the Constitution still lives in the structures it created. This is not to say that the freedoms of speech and religion and all the other protections guaranteed under the Bill of Rights are not important. But let us remember that the Constitution of 1787 protected slavery too and that the Bill of Rights had nothing to say about the modern conduct of war, the integration of public schools, or the conception of babies outside the womb. Community standards are too transient and controversial a notion upon which to base a government. In the end we have to put our trust in the rough-and-tumble of politics. To ensure that this rough-and-tumble would not create too radical a result, the framers created a political balance, which remains vital to this day. That system of balance is the part of the Constitution that lives. The adherence to and nurturing of that system through the protection of the process of representation and the promotion of the principle of process is the surest path to constitutional intent.

Notes
Index

Notes

1: Prerogative in American Politics

1. This issue came to a head with the signing of the Magna Carta and continued to be at issue through the rule of Henry VIII (in regard to the controversy concerning the Supremacy Act), the Puritan Revolution, and the execution of Charles I in 1649. One of the last acts of resistance against the prerogative powers of the king occurred in 1678 when King Charles II attempted, pursuant to his royal prerogative, to pardon Sir William Strafford for his role in the so-called Popish Plot. Parliament rejected the king's pardon and thus performed one of its last overt acts of resistance against the absolute power of the king prior to the establishment of a constitutional monarchy.

2. Circa 1758, Richard Bland, *Colonel Dismounted*, 26, quoted in Clinton Rossiter, *Seedtime of the Republic* (New York: Harcourt, Brace, 1953), 273.

3. Even so, English jurists recognized that there were constitutional limits on the exercise of the powers of parliament. Sir William Blackstone wrote: "Parliament is sometimes said to be 'omnipotent.' What is spoken of as the English Constitution embraces the body or system of laws, rules, principles and established usages, upon which is based the organization of the Government. . . . But this Constitution . . . has, by force of precedent, and by the natural effect of ordinary usage upon the habits and ideas of the people, great controlling and restrictive power upon the course of legislation." Sir William Blackstone, *Commentaries on the Laws of England* (New York: Banks and Brothers, 1895), 15, no. 7.

4. Henry Campbell Black, *Black's Law Dictionary* (St. Paul, Minn.: West, 1979), 1064.

5. John Locke, *Second Treatise of Government*, ed. C. B. Macpherson (Indianapolis: Hackett, 1980), 83.

6. See, for example, Arthur M. Schlesinger, *The Imperial Presidency* (New York: Popular Library, 1974); Richard M. Pious, *The American Presidency* (New York: Basic Books, 1979), 47–84; or Louis W. Koenig, *The Chief Executive*, 5th ed. (New York: Harcourt Brace Jovanovich, 1986), 11–12.

7. This predominant focus on the presidential prerogative is also a function of "scholars' normative preference for presidential strength in the 1950's and 1960's." See Michael Nelson, "Evaluating the Presidency," in *The Presidency and the Political System*, 2d ed., ed. Michael Nelson (Washington, D.C.: CQ

Press, 1988), 5–11; also Malcolm B. Parsons, "The Presidential Rating Game," in *The Future of the American Presidency,* ed. Charles Dunn (Morristown, N.J.: General Learning Press, 1975), 66–91.

8. Franz Neumann, *The Democratic and Authoritarian State* (Glencoe, Ill.: Free Press, 1957), 8.

9. 31 U.S.C. 665(c)(2).

10. It should be noted, however, that presidents have often been justly criticized for using so-called states of emergency to their own advantage. The power to declare a "state of emergency" is, in itself, a prerogative that is shared among the branches as will be discussed in chapters 3 and 4.

11. See, for example, Charles Hermann, "International Crisis as a Situational Variable," in *International Politics and Foreign Policy,* ed. James N. Rosenau (New York: Free Press, 1969), 409–21.

12. For a discussion of the meaning of "appropriate" consultation between the branches see U.S. Congress, House, Committee on Foreign Affairs, *Strengthening Executive-Legislative Consultation of Foreign Policy,* 97th Cong., 2d sess., October 1983.

13. Gerald Stourzh, *Alexander Hamilton and the Idea of Republican Government* (Stanford: Stanford University Press, 1970), 22.

14. Marbury v. Madison, 1 Cranch 137, 166 (1803).

15. One important exception in this respect is a short, straightforward discusson of presidential prerogative contained in Pious, *The American Presidency,* 48–84. By contrast, see Edward S. Corwin, *The President: Office and Powers, 1787–1957* (New York: New York University Press, 1957), 7–8, 147. Corwin is very reluctant to use the term "prerogative" in anything but the traditional Lockean sense and certainly *not* to refer to mainstream thought on the American presidency.

16. Locke's chapter on prerogative in the *Second Treatise* and the medieval tract *De Prerogative Regis* are good examples of this.

17. See Herbert Wechsler, "Towards Neutral Principles of Constitutional Law," *Harvard Law Review* 73 (1959): 1, for a discussion of the methods through which the courts arrive at a "principled" decision.

18. Complaints about the effects of extreme legalism in the United States have come from very disparate sources. Aleksandr Solzhenitsyn observed in his widely circulated Harvard commencement address that extreme legalism in the United States released Americans from the responsibility of having to act without any restraint other than absolute limits of the law. Therefore, when the law is not well defined or commonly understood, the limits of the law and, thus, the limits of behavior do not exist in a society that does not have any other way but the law to establish ethical standards. See "A World Split Apart," *The Wanderer* (4 July 1978): 5. Arthur Miller makes a similar argument when he suggests that the veneer of legalism allows the most powerful elements of society to manipulate the distribution of goods in society without alienating the less powerful segments of the populace. See Arthur Miller, ed., *Politics, Democracy, and the Supreme Court: Essays on the Frontier of Constitutional Theory* (Westport, Conn.: Greenwood Press, 1985), 41.

19. Walter Bagehot, *The English Constitution,* with an introduction by R. H. S. Crossman (Ithaca: Cornell University Press, 1986), 218. Bagehot sums up this problem in the next sentence: "The practical arguments and the legal

disquisitions in America are often like those of trustees carrying out a misdrawn will—the sense of what they mean is good, but it can never be worked out fully or defended simply, so hampered is it by the old words of an old testament."

20. Robert Nozick refers to this community as a "minimal state," or a society devoted exclusively to the protection, not redistribution, of property. See *Anarchy, State, and Utopia* (New York: Basic Books, 1974).

21. John Stuart Mill, *On Liberty*, ed. H. B. Acton (New York: Dutton, 1972), 132.

22. For a general discussion of this relationship, see John H. Herz, *International Politics in the Atomic Age* (New York: Columbia University Press, 1959), chaps. 1–6.

23. See, in particular, Madison's defense of the requirements of process as opposed to a dependence on "parchment barriers" for the protection of liberty in *The Federalist Papers*, ed. and with an introduction by Clinton Rossiter (New York: New American Library 1961), papers 47–51.

24. One suggestion for a reform of this type is advanced by Lloyd C. Cutler, "To Form a Government," *Foreign Affairs* 59 (Fall 1980): 126–43.

25. Woodrow Wilson, *Congressional Government* (Princeton: Princeton University Press, 1967), 17. See also Edward S. Corwin, "The Worship of the Constitution," *Constitutional Review* 4 (January 1920): 3.

2: The Transfer of Plenary Powers

1. For a thorough discussion of this, see Rossiter, *Seedtime of the Republic*, particularly 440–49.

2. See *Howell's State Trials*, 1083, cited in Francis Wormuth, *The Royal Prerogative: 1603–1649* (Port Washington, N.Y.: Kennikat, 1972), 55.

3. As James I wrote, "The state of monarchy is the supremest thing on earth; for kings are not only God's lieutenants on earth, but even by God himself they are called gods." Cited in Christopher Hill, *The Century of Revolution, 1603–1714*, 2d ed. (New York: Norton, 1980), 36.

4. For a discussion of this early conception of divided sovereignty, see Francis D. Wormuth, *The Origins of Modern Constitutionalism* (New York: Harper and Bros., 1949), chap. 4; or Edward S. Corwin, "The Higher Law Background of American Constitutional Law," *Harvard Law Review* 42 (1928): 149–85.

5. Sir Francis Bacon, *Essays and New Atlantis* (New York: Walter J. Black, 1942), 83.

6. Wormuth, *Origins of Modern Constitutionalism*, 54ff.

7. As John Seldin, lawyer and revolutionary parliamentarian said, "a king is a thing men have made for their own sakes, for quietness' sake. Just as in a family one man is appointed to buy the meat." Quoted in Hill, *Century of Revolution*, 36.

8. Prorogation was the prerogative of the British monarch to terminate a session of Parliament.

9. In 1625 Parliament attempted to refuse King Charles I the right to levy customs for life, limiting instead that grant of power to only one year. Charles I simply dissolved Parliament before a vote could be taken. The Petition of Right adopted by Parliament in 1628 only survived because it was presented to the

king as a "petition" rather than a Bill of Parliament. The king then had the prerogative to grant Parliament's petition, which he did not.

10. See Sir Robert Filmer, *Patriarcha*, with an introduction by Peter Laslitt (Oxford: Basil Blackwell, 1949). Filmer's absolutism became the straw man for attacks of antimonarchists such as Locke.

11. See F. J. Fisher, "The Sixteenth and Seventeenth Centuries: The Dark Ages in English Economic History," *Economica* 24 (1957): 289–306.

12. On this point see Sir John Eliot, *De Jure Majestatis* (Of the Rights of Sovereignty) a treatise written in 1629 while Eliot was awaiting execution in the Tower of London. Eliot argued for the supremacy of Parliament on ordinary matters, conceding however, in times of emergency the prerogative of the king to be supreme See also David Hume, *Essays Moral and Political*, for a later (1742) reiteration of the same theme.

13. In 1610, Justice Coke wrote in the Bonham case: "and it appears in our books, that in many cases, the common law will controul acts of Parliament, and sometimes adjudge them to be utterly void: for when an act of Parliament is against common right and reason, or repugnant, or impossible to be performed, the common law will controul it and adjudge such act to be void." Sir Edward Coke, 8 Co. 118a (1610), quoted in Edward S. Corwin, "The Higher Law Background of American Constitutional Law," *Harvard Law Review* 42 (1929): 368.

14. Thomas Jefferson said of Coke's writings:

With the lawyers it [support for England and the monarchy] is a new thing. They have, in the mother country, been generally the firmest supporters of the free principles of their constitution. But there too they have changed. I ascribe much of this to the substitution of Blackstone for my Lord Coke, as an elementary work.

"Thomas Jefferson in a letter to H. G. Spafford, 1814," quoted in Saul K. Padover, ed., *Thomas Jefferson on Democracy* (New York: New American Library, 1939), 84. Jefferson was referring to the fact that in Blackstone's *Commentaries*, Coke's notion of judicial review was rejected as a violation of legislative sovereignty. Jefferson went on to say about Blackstone in the same letter:

These two books [by Hume and Blackstone], but especially the former, have done more towards the suppression of the liberties of man, than all the million of men in arms of Bonaparte.

15. The fact that Filmer used as an analogy the parent-child relationship suggests that even he believed that some sort of mutual commitment existed between monarch and subject. Just as a parent has some kind of obligation for rearing a child, the king has some sort of obligation toward protecting his charges. Presumably, if one could accept the idea of a flawed exercise of parental authority, one could accept the idea of a flawed exercise of the king's prerogative. However, subjects could not do away with or deny their natural parentage. Similarly, subjects could no more choose their king than they could choose their parents. The social contract allowed for and justified revolt; paternalism and principle of noblesse oblige did not.

16. Thomas Hobbes, *Leviathan*, ed. and with an introduction by Francis B. Randall (New York: Washington Square Press, 1970), 118–19.

17. Locke, *Second Treatise*, 48.

18. Ibid., 49.

19. In actuality, the notion of a higher natural law was not a new one. Aristotle had discussed some form of natural law in his *Rhetoric* ("an unjust law is not a law"), as did Cicero in *De Legibus*. Thomas Aquinas argued in *Summa Theologica*, pt. 2, no. 3 that government actions beyond the law of nature were a perversion of law.

20. Locke, *Second Treatise*, 9.

21. Ibid., 86.

22. Ibid.

23. Thomas Jefferson, "Letter to Henry Lee, 1825," in Padover, *Thomas Jefferson on Democracy*, 13.

24. For an expansion of this notion of a conservative revolution, see Rossiter, *Seedtime of the Republic*.

25. See Bernard Bailyn, "The Logic of Rebellion," in *The Reinterpretation of the American Revolution: 1763–1769*, ed. Jack P. Greene (New York: Harper and Row, 1968), 228. The plight of the colonists was sometimes compared to the plight of the Jews in the Book of Esther with Lord North as Haman (the evil advisor to the king), George III as Ahasuerus (the remote and befuddled king), and the colonists as Esther and the Jews (ibid., 226).

26. On this point see Joseph Story, *Commentaries on the Constitution of the United States*, 4th ed. (Boston: Little, Brown, 1873), 129–31.

27. Pennsylvania is an important test case with regard to transition of the role of the executive and the development of political thought in the postrevolutionary era. Reformers such as Benjamin Rush argued that inasmuch as executive officials in state governments would serve at the pleasure of the people, the governor of a state would be an elected representative just like any other. An executive branch, which was essential to good government in any state, would then be permitted to exist even in a republic. This notion of executive as representative was in direct contrast to the character of the king's appointed governors who served as extensions of the king exercising the king's prerogative. See Gordon Wood, *The Creation of the American Republic, 1776–1787* (Chapel Hill: University of North Carolina Press, 1969), 438–46.

28. Congress recognized the inadequacy of the Articles from the beginning. Less than a week after the adoption of the Articles, Congress appointed a committee to determine how the plan could be improved.

29. For a discussion of the unsuitability of legislatures for the conduct of foreign affairs and; indeed, the tendency toward rashness in the actions of legislatures, see *Federalist* papers 64 by Jay and 48 by Madison in *Federalist Papers*, 390–95, 308–12.

30. "[T]hose entrusted with the executive power are not the masters of the people but its officers, whom it can establish and depose when it pleases, that there is no question for them of contracting but of obeying, and that in undertaking the functions which the State imposes on them, they are only fulfilling their duty as Citizens, without having any sort of right to dispute about the conditions." Jean-Jacques Rousseau, *Of the Social Contract*, with an introduction by Charles M. Sherover (New York: Harper and Row, 1984), 95–96.

31. Thomas Paine, *Common Sense* (Garden City, N.Y.: Dolphin Books, 1949), 26.

32. Many of the specifics of Rousseau's construct were wildly impractical.

For example, Rousseau had a great distaste for representative rule. Representatives, he believed, would become corrupted by their own personal motives. Furthermore, citizens in a representative republic would become complaisant about the activities of government. Therefore, the optimal form of social organization for Rousseau was the city-state—a place small enough so that all citizens could conveniently travel to meet at one time in the assembly. By the eighteenth century, however, the city-state was in most cases not viable. City-states could not defend themselves against the aggression of their imperial neighbors. Because of this problem and fear that the legislator would usurp dictatorial powers (as did Robespierre), much of what Rousseau had to say about governing was discredited. However, even liberal democrats owe a great debt to Rousseau's contribution. The idea that freedom would exist with (and, indeed, was the function of) restraint and that the social contract could be made flexible made it theoretically possible to build a viable, dynamic democracy.

33. Rousseau wrote in Of the Social Contract, "As nature gives each man an absolute power over all his limbs, the social pact gives the body politic an absolute power over all its members" (27).

34. Baron de Montesquieu, Spirit of the Laws, in The Political Theory of Montesquieu, ed. Melvin Richter (Cambridge: Cambridge University Press, 1977), 244.

35. Madison, writing to Philip Mazzei (10 December 1788), commented: "Philosophers on the old continent, in their zeal against tyranny, would rush into anarchy; as the horrors of superstition drive them into Atheism." Quoted in The Complete Madison, ed. Saul K. Padover (New York: Harper and Bros., 1953), 348.

36. Montesquieu does note the existence of "natural laws" (for example, humans eat when they are hungry). However, these laws should in no way be considered the equivalent of "natural rights" as discussed by other theorists of the time. See Montesquieu, Spirit of the Laws, 172–77.

37. For an exposition of this point, see The Federal Convention and the Formation of the Union of the American States, ed. and with an introduction by Winton U. Solberg (New York: Bobbs-Merrill, 1958), xxxix; and Francis D. Wormuth, The Royal Prerogative: 1603–1649, 116.

38. Quoted in Louis Fisher, President and Congress: Power and Policy (New York: Free Press, 1972), 255.

39. Federalist Papers, 401–2.

40. Quoted in Fisher, President and Congress, 257.

41. Hamilton wrote, "Every man the least conversant in Roman history knows how often that republic was obliged to take refuge in the absolute power of a single man, under the formidable title of dictator, as well against the intrigues of ambitious individuals who aspired to the tyranny, and the seditions of whole classes of the community whose conduct threatened the existence of all government, as against the invasions of external enemies who menaced the conquest and destruction of Rome." Federalist Papers, 423.

42. Federalist Papers, 435.

43. Hamilton said as much in regard to the presidential veto. In Federalist paper 69 he wrote: "to the necessity of exerting a prerogative which could seldom be exerted without hazarding some degree of national agitation. The

qualified negative of the President differs widely from the absolute negative of the British sovereign" (416–17).

44. On Wednesday, 12 September 1789, George Mason proposed that as a last act of the Constitutional Convention a committee be appointed to prepare a Bill of Rights to preface the Constitution. His motion was unanimously rejected, the general feeling being that the Constitution in no way repealed existing state declarations of rights. See James Madison, "Notes of Debates," in Solberg, *Federal Convention*, 331; in the same volume, see also Mason's objections, 335–38.

45. James Madison, "Letter to Thomas Jefferson, October 1788," in Padover, *Complete Madison*, 255.

46. Hamilton comes to the same conclusion in *Federalist* paper 84. See *Federalist Papers*, 510–20.

47. For a discussion of this point, see Thad Tate, "The Social Contract in America, 1774–1787," *William and Mary Quarterly* 22 (1965): 375–91.

3: Presidential Prerogative

1. Locke, *Second Treatise*, 83–84.

2. In a speech to his constituents in Bristol, England, Burke said: "Your representative owes you, not his industry only, but his judgement; and he betrays, instead of serving you, if he sacrifices it to your opinion." Edmund Burke, *Works of Edmund Burke* (Boston: Little, Brown, 1866), 2:95–96.

3. Edmund Burke, *Reflections on the Revolution in France* (Buffalo: Prometheus Books, 1987), 64. Interestingly, Madison writes in *Federalist* paper 10, "No man is allowed to be a judge in his own cause, because his interest would certainly bias his judgement, and, not improbably, corrupt his integrity." *Federalist Papers*, 9. One wonders if Burke who published his *Reflections* in 1790 was not "lifting" without citation Madison's wording in *Federalist* paper 10. Would it not be more accurate, then, to speak of Madisonian rather than Burkean representation?

4. Burke, *Reflections on the Revolution in France*, 64.

5. *Federalist Papers*, 82. For his part, Hamilton conceives of a very limited notion of natural rights. In *Federalist* paper 28 he recognizes the rights of individuals to self-defense through revolt against the state. However, in *Federalist* paper 78, he indicates that the Constitution, not natural right, is supreme. *Federalist Papers*, 180, 467–68.

6. "Letter from Thomas Jefferson to John Breckenridge, August 12, 1803," quoted in *The People Shall Judge: Readings in the Formation of American Policy*, ed. the Staff of the College of Social Sciences (Chicago: University of Chicago Press, 1949), 499.

7. *Federalist Papers*, 423.

8. *Federalist Papers*, 463–64. In concluding his discussion of the powers of the presidency, Hamilton devotes no more than a paragraph to the notion of controlling the executive. In that conclusion Hamilton suggests that periodic elections, impeachment provisions, and the countervailing force of Congress are adequate to the task of limiting presidential power. "What more can an enlightened and reasonable people desire?" he asks at the end of *Federalist* paper 77.

9. One must wonder, though, what the effect the Twenty-Second Amend-

ment (which limits the number of terms a president can serve to two) has on the representative quality of presidential rule.

10. One excellent example of this tendency is the defense of President Roosevelt's "Destroyer Deal." In 1940 Attorney General Robert H. Jackson defended President Roosevelt's decision to exchange American destroyers for military-base privileges with the British by making the rather absurd argument that under the Constitution the president, as commander-in-chief, can "dispose" of the armed forces of the United States. R. R. Jackson, "Acquisition of Naval and Air Bases in Exchange for Over-Age Destroyers," in *Official Opinions of the Attorneys General of the United States*, ed. J. T. Fowler (Washington: D.C.: U.S. G.P.O., 1941), 484–96.

11. William Howard Taft, "A Restricted View of the Office," in *Classics of the American Presidency*, ed. Harry A. Bailey (Oak Park, Ill.: Moore, 1980), 37.

12. See Myers v. U.S., 272 U.S. 52 (1926).

13. *The Gazette of the United States*, 18 September 1793, quoted in *The Constitution and American Foreign Policy*, ed. Jean Edward Smith (St. Paul, Minn.: West, 1989), 58.

14. This is being gentle. There is quite some scholarly literature to the effect that Madison was a rather poor president whose public career went into decline after the Constitutional Convention and the publishing of the *Federalist* papers. See, for instance, Edward McNall Burns, *James Madison: Philosopher of the Constitution* (New Brunswick, N.J.: Rutgers, 1938) or J. C. A. Stagg, *Mr. Madison's War: Politics, Diplomacy, and Warfare in the Early American Republic, 1783–1830* (Princeton: Princeton University Press, 1983).

15. For an excellent discussion of the environmental incentives that may drive a president to bypass Congress, see Bruce Buchanan, *The Presidential Experience: What the Office Does to the Man* (Englewood Cliffs, N.J.: Prentice-Hall, 1978), chap. 6. For a thorough discussion of the correlates of presidential success as perceived by modern scholars, see Dean Keith Simonton, *Why Presidents Succeed* (New Haven: Yale University Press, 1987) especially chap. 5. It seems that besides external variables that seem to determine presidential success (such as war), successful presidents (i.e., those ranked highly in surveys by modern historians) have a "will to power" that dictates an aggressive strategy when dealing with Congress.

16. Theodore Roosevelt, "The Stewardship Doctrine," in Bailey, *Classics of the American Presidency*, 35.

17. Smith, *The Constitution and American Foreign Policy*, 53.

18. Martin v. Mott, 12 Wheaton (25 U.S.) 19, 30 (1827).

19. Prize Cases, 2 Black (67 U.S.) 635, 668 (1862).

20. Ibid., at 671.

21. *Ex parte* Milligan, 4 Wallace (71 U.S.) 2 (1866). The Court's decision in the Milligan case was a departure from a decision rendered by the Court just three years earlier in the case of *Ex parte* Vallandigham, 1 Wallace (68 U.S.) 243 (1863). In that case a man had been tried and convicted by a military court in Ohio. The Supreme Council refused to review his conviction. The difference between these two cases is an important example of the difference between those decisions made in wartime and those made in peacetime.

22. *New York Times* v. United States, 403 U.S. 713, 715–19 (1971). It

should be noted that Justice Black, along with Justice Douglas, made a very broad constitutional case in support of the Court's decision. By contrast, in separate, concurring decisions, Justices Stewart and White together, and Justice Marshall on his own found in favor of the newspaper on much narrower grounds, leaving the door open for future adjudication on these issues. Justices Harlan, Burger, and Blackmun dissented.

23. National Security Act of 1947, 50 U.S.C. 401, section 102(d)(3).

24. C.I.A. v. Sims, 471 U.S. 159 (1985).

25. Youngstown Co. v. Sawyer, 343 U.S. 579, 662 (1952).

26. Korematsu v. United States, 323 U.S. 214 (1944). On 10 August 1988 President Reagan signed into law PL 100–383, a bill to provide reparations for the losses suffered by Japanese-Americans interned during World War II. The bill included an apology and earmarked $1.25 billion for payments to survivors.

27. Justice Black wrote: "He [Korematsu] was excluded because we are at war with the Japanese Empire, because the properly constituted military authorities feared an invasion of our West Coast and felt constrained to take proper security measures . . . and finally, because Congress, reposing its confidence in time of war in our military leaders—as it inevitably must—determined that they had the power to do just this." This is not a clear endorsement of unrestrained executive power in wartime but it seems that war, not Congress's recognition of war, creates these dramatic presidential powers.

28. See Ex parte Quirin, 317 U.S. 1 (1942); or In re Yamashita, 327 U.S. 1 (1946).

29. Ex parte Quirin, 317 U.S. 1, 26 (1942).

30. Presidential Proclamation 2714, 12 Fed. Reg. 1. The proclamation recognized that "a state of war still exists."

31. Woods v. Miller, 333 U.S. 138, 142 (1948). Another important precedent in this regard is the Court's ruling in Hamilton v. Kentucky Distilleries Co., 251 U.S. 146 (1919). In that case, the Court ruled that the wartime Prohibition Act could be extended beyond the armistice that ended World War I.

32. 84 Cong. Rec. 2854 (1939).

33. Richard Pious identifies over 400 statutes of this kind. See Pious, The American Presidency, 216.

34. PL 99–93, 99 Stat. 448.

35. United States v. Curtiss-Wright Export Corp., 299 U.S. 304, 320 (1936).

36. Durand v. Hollins, Fed. Cas. 111 (No. 4186)(C.C.S.D.N.Y.1860).

37. The official justification for the invasion of Grenada in 1983 was for the protection of 595 U.S. medical students living on the island who were supposedly endangered by an insurrection. The fact that at the same time as U.S. forces were protecting American lives the ruling Marxist regime was overthrown was incidental to the invasion. See the text of President Reagan's address to the nation in New York Times, 28 October 1983, A9.

38. For example it was discovered by the Senate Foreign Relations committee that during the Vietnam War, with the full knowledge of both Thai and American officials, a plan was agreed upon whereby American troops would come to the defense of Thailand in case of communist attack (COMUSTAF plan 1/64).

39. United States v. Belmont, 301 U.S. 324, 330 (1937). Also in reference

to executive agreements see Justice Douglas's decision in United States v. Pink, 315 U.S. 203, 229 (1942).

40. United States v. Guy W. Capps, 204 F.2d 655 (4th Cir. 1953).

41. Reid v. Covert, 354 U.S. 1 (1957).

42. Some 87 percent of all executive agreements negotiated between 1946 and 1972 were defined as agreements entered into pursuant to existing legislation. The rest can only be described as exercises of pure presidential prerogative. See Lock Johnson and James M. McCormick, "The Making of International Agreements: A Reappraisal of Congressional Involvement," *Journal of Politics* 40 (May 1978): 473.

43. Article 1, section 7.

44. Between 1789 and 1987, the pocket veto was applied 1040 times. See Robert J. Spitzer, *The Presidential Veto: Touchstone of the American Presidency* (Albany: State University of New York Press, 1988), 72.

45. Kennedy v. Sampson, 511 F 2d 430 [D.C. Cir. 1974].

46. Burke v. Barnes, 93 L Ed 2d 732.

47. See Chuck Alston, "Bush Crusades on Many Fronts to Retake President's Turf," *Congressional Quarterly Weekly Report* 48 (3 February 1990): 293.

48. For a more complete discussion of the pocket veto controversy, see Spitzer, *The Presidential Veto*, 105–19.

49. As a matter of practice, congressional appropriations committees demand prior consultation as regards the reprogramming of funds. Executive agencies have an incentive to consult Congress, inasmuch as an attempt to bypass Congress through the reprogramming of funds could result in the loss of discretionary power for the agency. There have been attempts, however (particularly on the part of the Department of Defense) to use reprogramming as a way to circumvent congressional intent. See Louis Fisher, *The Politics of Shared Power: Congress and the Executive*, 2d ed. (Washington, D.C.: Congressional Quarterly Press, 1987), 89–92.

50. The reprogramming of funds may only take place within a budget account. See Fisher, *President and Congress*, 118.

51. *In re* Neagle, 135 U.S. 1, 59 (1890). According to this and other judicial precedents, the president has enormous leeway to protect the "peace" of the nation. See also Moyer v. Peabody, 212 U.S. 78 (1909).

52. For example, Thomas Jefferson impounded funds intended for the building of gunboats on the Mississippi River. Between the time the money was appropriated and the money was to be spent, the Louisiana Purchase obviated the need for gunboats to patrol what was no longer an international boundary. President Jefferson withheld those funds from expenditure. The funds, however, were eventually spent. It has been reported that Jefferson insisted on designing those gunboats himself. His prototype capsized and sank during trials and he used the Louisiana Purchase as an excuse to delay the expenditure of funds while he redid the design. See Vivian Vale, "The Obligation to Spend: Presidential Impoundment of Congressional Appropriations," *Political Studies* 25 (December 1977): 513.

53. See, for example, Local 2677 v. Phillips, 358 F.Supp. 60 (D.D.C. 1973). In that case, the court ruled that the executive could not use impoundments as an excuse not to enforce laws with which it disagreed. In State Highway Commission of Missouri v. Volpe, 347 F.Supp. 950 (W.D.Mo. 1972), the court held

that highway funds could not be withheld for the purpose of countering inflation and in Train v. City of New York 420 U.S. 35 (1975), the court rejected the argument that Congress had granted the executive broad authority to withhold funds designated for cleaning up polluted rivers. In other words, according to Laurence Tribe, "monies appropriated to clean up dirty rivers might be impounded by the President because there were no more dirty rivers; they could not be impounded to stabilize the consumer price index." Laurence Tribe, *American Constitutional Law* (Mineola, N.Y.: Foundation Press, 1978), 196ff.

54. See the Economic Stabilization Act of 1970, 84 Stat. 799, or the Budget and Impoundment Control Act of 1974, PL 93–344, Title X.

55. While the courts have recognized as proper increasingly broad delegations of authority to the executive, the nondelegation doctrine still survives. See, for example, Industrial Union v. American Petroleum, 448 U.S. 607 (1980).

56. United States v. Nixon, 418 U.S. 683 (1974).

57. Richard Nathan, a former political appointee, has written that "there is still a strong, almost wistful, feeling on the part of some public administration specialists and old-line career officials that political officials should stay out of administrative processes." *The Administrative Presidency* (New York: John Wiley and Sons, 1983), 6.

58. Between 1936 and 1983 the number of pages in the *Federal Register* increased from 2,355 to 57,703. Norman Ornstein, et al., *Vital Statistics on Congress, 1984–1985 Edition* (Washington, D.C.: American Enterprise Institute, 1984), 151.

59. For an excellent case study on this point, see Jeffrey L. Pressman and Aaron B. Wildavsky, *Implementation* (Berkeley: University of California Press, 1973).

60. Department secretaries average about forty months on the job while at the subcabinet level, the average tenure has been about eighteen months. See Hugh Heclo, *A Government of Strangers: Executive Politics in Washington* (Washington, D.C.: Brookings Institution, 1977), 103.

61. There is a vast amount of scholarly literature concerning the capture of bureaucratic organizations and the establishment of "iron triangles." Some of the more prominent publications in this genre are Samuel Huntington, "The Marasmus of the ICC," *Yale Law Journal* 61 (April 1952): 467–509; Gabriel Kolko, *Railroads and Regulation* (Princeton: Princeton University Press, 1965); Grant McConnell, *Private Power and American Democracy* (New York: Knopf, 1966). The concept of the iron triangle is probably oversimplified. In fact, there seems to be quite a bit of fragmentation in the politics of iron triangles. On this point see Erwin G. Krasnow et al., *The Politics of Broadcast Regulation*, 3d ed. (New York: St. Martin's, 1982).

62. See Graham Allison, *Essence of Decision: Explaining the Cuban Missile Crisis* (Boston: Little, Brown, 1971), 141–42; and Morton Halperin, *Bureaucratic Politics and Foreign Policy* (Washington, D.C.: Brookings Institution, 1974), 241–42.

63. PL 79–404.

64. See U.S. Congress, House, Committee on Energy and Commerce, Subcommittee on Oversight and Investigations, *OMB: The Role of the Office of Management and Budget in Regulation*, 97th Cong., 1st sess., 19 June 1981.

65. The EOP staff numbered 2,755 in 1960, increasing to 5,722 in 1972.

Much of this growth came in divisions of the Executive Office (the National Security Council and the Office of Management and Budget) directly concerned with the president's prerogative in domestic and international affairs. See Harold Relyea, "Organizing the Presidency: The Administrative Presidency," in *The American Presidency: A Policy Perspective from Readings and Documents,* ed. David Kozak and Kenneth Ciboski (Chicago: Nelson-Hall, 1988), 105–48.

66. There are a number of reasons that RARG was thought to be less than successful. For example, it was never entirely clear that the group's review of selected agency regulations was comprehensive enough. For more on this, see Susan Tolchin, "Presidential Power and the Politics of RARG," *Regulation* (July–August 1979): 45.

67. Executive Order 12291, 17 February 1981. The twenty-two independent regulatory agencies in the federal government were excluded from the president's order but were asked to voluntarily comply.

68. See Susan J. Tolchin and Martin Tolchin, *Dismantling America: The Rush to Deregulate* (New York: Oxford University Press, 1983), 70. Tolchin and Tolchin, however, question whether this effort to control regulation has been truly successful inasmuch as "presidential 'management' has led to decreased protection from the harmful effects of advancing technologies" (71).

69. Jefferey K. Tulis, *The Rhetorical Presidency* (Princeton: Princeton University Press, 1987).

70. Ibid., 25–59.

71. Ibid., 117–54.

72. House Document 834, quoted in Richard A. Watson and Norman C. Thomas, *The Politics of the Presidency,* 2d ed. (Washington, D.C.: Congressional Quarterly Press, 1988), 460.

73. See, for example, President Bush's reaction to the Fiscal Year 1990–1991 State Department Authorization Bill in John Felton, "Bush Throws Down the Gauntlet on Provisions He Opposes." *Congressional Quarterly Weekly Report* 48 (24 February 1990): 603–4.

4: Congressional Prerogative

1. "Construction" is the judicial process in which the courts may rely on evidence beyond the text of the law, including "probable aim" or "purpose" of a provision. In this sense, construction is different from "interpretation" to the extent that the court must go beyond the text of the Constitution or statute in order to arrive at a determination. In a more general sense, therefore, construction could be considered the process through which the prerogative powers of government have developed through the courts. See *McKinney's Consolidated Laws of New York, Book 1* (St. Paul, Minn.: West, 1971), 138–39, for a more thorough discussion of the concept of construction as understood by the courts. See also Joseph Story, *Commentaries on the Constitution,* chap. 5, on "Rules of Interpretation."

2. For example, it has been suggested that the separation of powers be bridged by some sort of parliamentary reform. See, for example, Cutler, "To Form a Government"; and U.S. Congress, House, Committee on Banking, Finance and Urban Affairs, *Looking Towards the Bicentennial—A Proposed Amendment to Permit Members of Congress to Serve in Key Executive Branch*

Offices, 96th Cong., 1st sess., January 1980. In such cases the legislative branch would be part of the actual decision-making process itself.

3. Anderson v. Dunn, 6 Wheat. 204 (1821). The Court ruled, however, that a prisoner imprisoned on a contempt of Congress charge could not be held beyond the adjournment date of Congress.

4. 2 U.S.C. 192.

5. Kilbourn v. Thompson, 103 U.S. 168, 190 (1881).

6. McGrain v. Daugherty, 273 U.S. 135, 173 (1927).

7. Watkins v. United States, 354 U.S. 178, 206 (1957).

8. Barenblatt v. United States, 360 U.S. 109, 127 (1959).

9. See Arthur M. Schlesinger, Jr., *The Imperial Presidency.*

10. See Norman J. Ornstein, Thomas E. Mann, and Michael J. Malbin, *Vital Statistics on Congress, 1989–1990* (Washington, D.C.: Congressional Quarterly Inc., 1990), 132 and 136 respectively.

11. Ibid., 140–41.

12. Ibid., 203–4.

13. In 1987, the president's "support score" in Congress was 43.7 percent according to *Congressional Quarterly Weekly Reports.* President Reagan was the first president since 1953, the year that *Congressional Quarterly* began its voting studies, to fall below a 50 percent success rate. In 1988, the president's success score was slightly higher, 47.4 percent. See Chuck Alston, "Reagan's Support Index Up—But Not Much," *Congressional Quarterly Weekly Reports* (19 November 1988): 3323–30.

14. For general discussions concerning congressional assertiveness particularly in foreign policy in the 1970s and 1980s, see Frans R. Bax, "The Legislative-Executive Relationship in Foreign Policy: New Partnership or New Competition," *Orbis* 20 (Winter 1977): 881–904; Thomas M. Franck and Edward Weisband, *Foreign Policy by Congress* (New York: Oxford University Press, 1979); or, for a recent case study, I. M. Destler, "The Elusive Congress: Congress and Central America," in *Central America,* ed. Robert S. Leiken (New York: Pergamon, 1984).

15. See Bob Woodward, *Veil: The Secret Wars of the CIA, 1981–1987* (New York: Simon and Schuster, 1987).

16. Yakus v. United States, 321 U.S. 414, 442–443 (1944).

17. Schenk v. United States, 249 U.S. 47, 52 (1919).

18. See, for example, Texas v. Johnson, U.S.L.W. 57 (20 June 1989): 4770–81.

19. United States v. Macintosh, 283 U.S. 605, 622 (1931).

20. Home Building and Loan Association v. Blaisdell, 290 U.S. 398 (1934).

21. These are the examples that Justice Hughes relied on.

22. Home Building and Loan Association v. Blaisdell, 290 U.S. 398 (1934), 426.

23. Locke, *Second Treatise,* 180.

24. See U.S. House of Representatives, Committee on Foreign Affairs, *Strengthening Executive-Legislative Consultation on Foreign Policy,* 1.

25. There are a variety of definitions, forms, and functional equivalents of the legislative veto. "Report and wait" provisions, for example, are requirements that administrative agencies make a report of their intentions to act, which then must be approved by some portion (one house, one committee) of Congress

before the agency executes the law. Similarly, certain "negative" legislative vetoes require that Congress act to approve an administrative action within a
certain time period. If Congress fails to act, the agency's decision is automatically
disapproved. For example, presidential rescissions must be approved by Congress (by joint resolution, presidential signature required) within 45 days or the
funds impounded must be automatically released. Also, the War Powers Resolution requires that Congress approve certain types of armed interventions
within 60 days or, congressional approval not forthcoming, withdraw those
troops within 90 days. It is probable that the Chadha decision did not affect
these forms of legislative vetoes. See Daniel Paul Franklin, "Why the Legislative
Veto Isn't Dead," *Presidential Studies Quarterly* 16 (Summer 1986): 491–502.

26. 53 Stat. 561.

27. Section 244(c)(2).

28. INS v. Chadha, 462 U.S. 919. Art. 1, sect. 7 of the Constitution requires
that "every Bill which shall have passed the House of Representatives and the
Senate shall, before it become a Law, be *presented* to the President of the United
States."

29. Two weeks after Chadha, the Court affirmed a lower court's ruling that
struck down a two-house veto of a Federal Trade Commission regulation in
Consumers Union, Inc. v. FTC, 691 F.2d 575 (D.C. Cir. 1982). Also, the courts
struck down two other one-house veto provisions in Consumer Energy Council
of America v. FERC, 463 U.S. 1216 (1983) and City of New Haven, Conn. v.
U.S., 809 F.2d 900 (D.C. Cir. 1987).

30. See Louis Fisher, "Legislative Vetoes Enacted After Chadha," Report
87–388 (Washington, D.C.: Congressional Research Service, 1987).

31. See Louis Fisher, "Judicial Misjudgments About the Lawmaking Process: The Legislative Veto Case," in *Congress and Public Policy: A Source Book
of Documents and Readings,* 2d ed., ed. David C. Kozak and John D. Macartney
(Chicago: Dorsey, 1987), 425–34 for a discussion of the reasons why and ways
in which the legislative veto has survived the Chadha ruling. A recent and prominent example of an informal legislative veto provision is Secretary of State James
Baker's assurance to congressional leaders that aid authorized by Congress in
previous legislation (PL 101–14) to Nicaraguan contras would be cleared pe-
riodically with eight members of the congressional leadership before being transmitted. See John Felton, "Hill Gives Contra Package Bipartisan Launching,"
Congressional Quarterly Weekly Report 47 (15 April 1989): 832–36.

32. 22 U.S.C. 2422 Sec. 662.

33. This reporting requirement is still a subject of controversy. On 30 October 1989 President Bush wrote a letter to Senator Boren (D.-Okla.), chairman
of the Senate Select Intelligence Committee. In that letter, the president spelled
out what he considered to be his obligations under the law to report covert
operations to the committee. While the president recognized the right of the
committee to be informed "in a timely fashion of intelligence operations in
foreign countries," he asserted that "a number of factors combine to support
the conclusion that the "timely fashion" language should be read to leave the
President with virtually unfettered discretion to choose the right moment for
making the required notification." The president concluded that "any with-
holding . . . would be based upon my assertion of the authorities granted this
office by the Constitution."

34. For more on this see John R. Johannes, "Study and Recommend: Statutory Reporting Requirements as a Technique of Legislative Initiative—A Research Note," *Western Political Quarterly* (December 1976): 589–96.

35. The relationship between members of Congress and the administrative state are so close as to call into question the meaning of the constitutional recognition of the president as chief executive. In fact, some observers have suggested that, in the aftermath of decentralization in Congress, the relationship between members and bureaucrats is so profound that the oversight function of Congress is being subverted by the mutual dependence of members who supply appropriations and bureaucrats who allocate those funds. See, for example, Lawrence C. Dodd and Richard L. Schott, *Congress and the Administrative State* (New York: John Wiley and Sons, 1979), chap. 5; and Morris P. Fiorina, "Flagellating the Federal Bureaucracy," in *The Political Economy: Readings in the Politics and Economics of American Public Policy,* ed. Thomas Ferguson and Joel Rogers (New York: M. E. Sharpe, 1984), 224–34.

36. PL 93–344, 31 U.S.C. 1301.

37. As discussed in chapter 3, President Bush has attempted to counter this omnibus approach by asserting his authority to interpret the enforceability of legislation through his signing of statements and other administrative actions.

38. See David Rapp, "Negotiators Agree on Outlines of Fiscal 1990 Plan," *Congressional Quarterly Weekly Report* 47 (15 April 1989): 804–5.

39. For example, Miller and Stokes demonstrate that on foreign-policy issues, most members of Congress are willing to follow the president's lead. See Warren E. Miller and Donald E. Stokes, "Constituency Influence in Congress," *American Political Science Review* 57 (March 1963): 45–57.

40. On this point see, for example, Ryan J. Barilleaux, "The President, 'Intermestic' Issues, and the Risks of Policy Leadership," *The Domestic Sources of American Foreign Policy,* ed. Charles Kegley and Eugene Wittkopf (New York: St. Martin's, 1988), 178–88.

41. There are any number of works that discuss the causes and effects of decentralization in Congress. See James Sundquist, *The Decline and Resurgence of Congress* (Washington, D.C.: Brookings Institution, 1981); Lawrence C. Dodd and Bruce I. Oppenheimer, "The House in Transition," in *Congress Reconsidered,* 1st ed., ed. Dodd and Oppenheimer (New York: Praeger, 1977), 27–32; and Roger H. Davidson and Walter J. Oleszek, *Congress Against Itself* (Bloomington: Indiana University Press, 1977). The most important changes of the reform era were the requirements that a member could chair no more than one subcommittee at a time and that a chairmanship of a standing committee or of an appropriations subcommittee could be challenged by secret ballot in the party caucus. These changes had the effect of transferring the power of committees into the approximately 150 subcommittees of the House.

42. For example, decentralization seems to have had the effect of strengthening the relationship between subcommittee chairs, federal agencies, and lobbyists, the so-called iron triangles. See Dodd and Schott, *Congress and the Administrative State.* Thus, President Reagan complained in his farewell address on domestic politics (13 December 1988): "It sometimes seems to many Americans that what might be called a triangle of institutions—parts of Congress, the media, and special interest groups—is transforming and placing out of focus our constitutional balance, particularly in areas of spending and foreign policy."

President Reagan's emphasis on "the media" deviates from traditional notions of the iron triangle. However, he can be forgiven this oversight inasmuch as this address was delivered to thousands of his own appointments to the bureaucracy. Also, his vetoes of the "Whistleblower Protection Act of 1988" (S 508) and of the "Post-Employment Restrictions Act of 1988" (HR 5043) can be taken as indication of his incomplete acceptance of mainstream theories of the iron triangle. See A. Lee Fitschler, *Smoking and Politics* (New York: Appleton-Century-Crofts, 1969); and Norman J. Ornstein and Shirley Elder, *Interest Groups, Lobbying and Policymaking* (Washington, D.C.: Congressional Quarterly Press, 1978) for, respectively, a case study and a general discussion of lobbying in Congress and the bureaucracy.

43. See Sundquist, *Decline and Resurgence of Congress.*

44. It should also be noted that not all congressional reforms in the 1970s contributed to the decentralization of power. In 1975 the House Democratic Party Caucus authorized the Speaker to appoint, subject to party approval, all of the Democratic members of the Rules Committee. Thus, the Rules Committee becomes a tool of the majority party. In the Senate, the use of the cloture rule (Rule 22) to limit debate has increased dramatically in the 1970s and 1980s. Rule 22 was amended in 1975 to allow for a three-fifths rather than a two-thirds vote to end debate. See Walter J. Oleszek, "Legislative Procedures and Congressional Policymaking: A Bicameral Perspective," in *Congressional Politics,* ed. Christopher J. Deering (Chicago: Dorsey, 1989), 176–96.

45. The Government Operations Committee in the House is responsible, along with the General Accounting Office, for overseeing the execution of legislative intent. In addition, a number of substantive committees in both houses of Congress have established oversight subcommittees designated for the same purpose.

46. A recent administration challenge to the special prosecutor law was turned down by the Supreme Court. See Chief Justice Rehnquist's decision in Morrison v. Olson, 56 U.S.L.W. 4835 (1988).

47. Thomas Jefferson wrote in 1816: "Some men look at constitutions with sanctimonious reverence and deem them like the ark of the covenant, too sacred to be touched. . . . But I know also that laws and institutions must go hand in hand with the progress of the human mind." Quoted from a letter to Kercheval in Padover, *Thomas Jefferson on Democracy,* 153.

5 : Exploring the Judicial Prerogative

1. 77 Eng. Rep. 646, 652 (1610). Quoted in Edward S. Corwin, "The Supreme Court and Unconstitutional Acts of Congress," in *Corwin on the Constitution,* ed. Richard Loss (Ithaca: Cornell University Press, 1987), 2:43.

2. See note 12, chapter 2.

3. City of London v. Wood, 88 Eng. Rep. 1592 (1702).

4. Quoted in Story, *Commentaries on the Constitution,* 132.

5. See Wood, *Creation of the American Republic,* 160–61.

6. Governor Hutchinson of Massachusetts in summarizing the prevailing sentiment against the Stamp Act argued that it was, "against the Magna Carta and the natural rights of Englishmen, and therefore, according to Lord Coke,

null and void." See Corwin, "The Debt of American Constitutional Law to Natural Law Concepts" in Loss, *Corwin on the Constitution*, 1:199.

7. One of the most important preconvention cases in this regard was the case of Rutgers v. Waddington. Waddington, an agent for British merchants, had used Rutgers's abandoned property during the British occupation of New York City. According to the law of nations recognized under the New York State constitution, abandoned property could be used during wartime when authorized by a local military commander. However, the New York State legislature passed the Trespass Act of 1783 under which Rutgers sued for compensation. The Mayor's Court in New York City ruled that since the Trespass Act did not repeal the law of nations, Waddington was protected against prosecution.

8. "America had a long tradition of extra-legislative action by the people, action that more often than not had taken the form of mob violence and crowd disturbance." Wood, *Creation of the American Republic*, 319.

9. See Madison's remarks in *Federalist* papers 47 and 52, *Federalist Papers*, 300–308, 324–25.

10. Montesquieu, *Spirit of the Laws*, Bk. 11, chap. 6, 245.

11. Ibid.

12. James Madison, "Notes of Debates in the Federal Convention," reprinted in Solberg, *Federal Convention*, 230.

13. The compromise text was "a Republican form of Government shall be guaranteed to each State and that each State shall be protected against foreign and domestic violence." This resolution passed unanimously. Madison, reprinted in Solberg, *Federal Convention*, 231.

14. Ibid., 226.

15. Art. 4, sect. 1. Hamilton commented on this provision, "next to permanency in office, nothing can contribute more to the independence of judges than a fixed provision for their support." *Federalist* paper 79, *Federalist Papers*, 472.

16. This idea had been proposed earlier (May 29) by Edmund Randolph as part of the Virginia Plan. Randolph's plan for a "Council of Revision" was amended on June 4 to exclude the judiciary from the exercise of the veto power. Only the president was to exercise the veto. The general objection to the measure was *not* that judges would have the power to overrule acts of the legislature but that by furnishing the judiciary with part of the veto power, the separation of powers structure would be violated. How could judges be asked at the same time to be part of the policy-making and adjudication process? To have the judiciary as part of the policy-making process would be to bias their decisions in ruling on the applicability of the law. According to Madison's notes on the Constitutional Convention, Elbridge Gerry remarked in passing that some state judges already had the power to set aside laws as being against the Constitution. See Solberg, *Federal Convention*, 78, 96–101.

17. Ibid., 240.

18. Art. 3, sect. 2.

19. Art. 6, clause 2 of the Constitution reads: "This Constitution, and the laws of the United States which shall be made in Pursuance thereof; and all Treaties made, or which shall be made, under the Authority of the United States, shall be the supreme Law of the Land; and the Judges in every State shall be

bound thereby, any Thing in the Constitution or Laws of any State to the Contrary notwithstanding."

20. *Federalist Papers*, 467.

21. On this point, Corwin believed that there is no indication that either Madison *or* Hamilton initially believed that the power of the courts applied to Congress. He cites Hamilton's argument in *Federalist* paper 80 to support his conclusion. What Corwin thought of *Federalist* paper 78 in this regard is hard to know but it is clear that Hamilton was not necessarily discussing the acts of *state* legislatures in *Federalist* paper 78. Therefore, it is not too bold to suggest that Hamilton presaged the development of judicial review as we understand it today. See Corwin, "The Establishment of Judicial Review," in Loss, *Corwin on the Constitution*, 2:55.

Eventually, during the debate in Congress over the adoption of the Bill of Rights, Madison came to the conclusion that the power of judicial review was the only way to protect individual liberties under the Constitution. See James Madison's speech to the House of Representatives, 8 June 1789, *Annals of the U.S. Congress* (1789–91), 1:440–60.

22. For further information on this see Russell Wheeler, "Extrajudicial Activities of the Early Supreme Court," in *Supreme Court Review, 1973*, ed. Phillip B. Kurland (Chicago: University of Chicago Press, 1974), 123–58; and Robert Scigliano, "The Presidency and the Judiciary," in Nelson, *The Presidency and the Political System*, 435–61.

23. See Hayburn's case, 2 U.S. (2 Dall.) 409 (1792).

24. Justice Chase wrote in one such case: "it is unnecessary at this point for me to determine whether this court constitutionally possesses the power to declare an act of congress void on the ground of its being contrary to . . . the Constitution, but if the court have such power, I am free to declare, that I will never exercise it but in a very clear case." See Hylton v. United States, 3 Dall. 171 (1796); and Ware v. Hylton, 3 Dall. 199 (1796).

25. On 21 July 1787 during the debates of the Constitutional Convention James Madison, in support of the second resolution to establish some kind of council of revision, commented: "Experience in all the States had evinced a powerful tendency in the Legislature to absorb all power into its vortex. This was the real source of danger to the American Constitutions." "Notes of Debates," in Solberg, *Federal Convention*, 236. It is interesting to note that Madison's notes were not published until 1840. Therefore, during this period, the proceedings of the convention remained somewhat a mystery for those who were not there. In addition, those who were at the convention had the luxury of changing their views without being vulnerable to the charge of inconsistency.

26. The only type of suit that can be brought against a state in federal court is one in which one state sues another state or in the event that the U.S. government is a party to the suit. This amendment also does not prohibit citizens from bringing a case to federal court on appeal from a state court.

27. Chisholm v. Georgia, 2 U.S. (2 Dall.) 419 (1793).

28. See Lawrence H. Tribe, *American Constitutional Law*, 130.

29. Art. 3, sect. 1.

30. Corwin also makes the point that by this time the French Revolution had had a sobering effect on those who believed that the "people" could be trusted in a democracy. Increasingly, the courts were seen as a structure in which

society could be saved from itself. See Corwin, "The Establishment of Judicial Review," In Loss, *Corwin on the Constitution*, 2:67ff.

31. The Supreme Court was enlarged from five members to seven in 1802.

32. 1 Stat. 73, sect. 13. A writ of mandamus commands the performance of a specific act or duty.

33. Marbury v. Madison, 1 Cranch 137, 177–78 (1803).

34. The same day that Chase was impeached in the House, another federal judge, John Pickering of New Hampshire, was removed from office by the Senate. The Pickering impeachment, however, was not an applicable test case, as he had gone insane while on the bench. See Gerald Gunther, *Cases and Materials on Constitutional Law* (Mineola, N.Y.: Foundation Press, 1975), 14.

35. Although the Court continued to declare state laws unconstitutional. See Fletcher v. Peck, 6 Cranch 87 (1810), for example.

36. Dred Scott v. Sandford, 19 Howard 393 (1857).

37. See Thomas Geoghegan, "Warren Court Children," *New Republic* 194 (19 May 1986): 17–23.

38. Only twelve cabinet appointments in American history, including Sen. John Tower's appointment as Secretary of Defense, have been rejected. Twenty-nine Supreme Court nominees, including Ginsburg and Bork, have been rejected by the Senate.

39. See Pollock v. Farmers Loan and Trust Co., 157 U.S. 429 (1895).

40. Oregon v. Mitchell 400 U.S. 112 (1970).

41. Art. 3, sect. 1 of the Constitution delegates the responsibility of regulating the lower courts to Congress: "The judicial Power of the United States, shall be vested in one Supreme Court, and in such inferior Courts as the Congress may from time to time ordain and establish." Article 3 is interpreted, as well, to mean that Congress can regulate the jurisdiction of the federal courts, including the Supreme Court. Art. 3, sect. 2 reads, in part: "In all the other cases before mentioned, the Supreme Court shall have appellate jurisdiction, both as to law and fact, *with such exceptions and under such regulations as the Congress shall make.*"

42. See Henry Hart, "The Power of Congress to Limit the Jurisdiction of Federal Courts: An Exercise in Dialectic," *Harvard Law Review* 66 (1953): 1362.

43. *Ex parte* McCardle, 6 Wall. 318 (1868).

44. 15 Stat. 44.

45. *Ex parte* McCardle, 7 Wall. 506 (1869).

46. See Klein v. Wall, 128 (1872). There is some question as to whether, in altering the courts' jurisdiction, Congress may interfere with an individual's access to protection under the Bill of Rights. See Justice Rutledge's dissent in Yakus v. United States, 321 U.S. 414, 468 (1944).

47. See Tribe, *American Constitutional Law*, 33–47.

48. See 42 U.S.C.A. as amended. Also see The Emergency Price Control Act (56 Stat. 23).

49. Tribe, *American Constitutional Law*, 44–47.

50. 28 U.S.C. 1471.

51. 458 U.S. 50 (1982).

52. There are three circumstances in which Congress can establish Article 3 legislative courts (1) Congress can establish "territorial courts" in U.S. pos-

sessions outside the fifty states; 2) Congress and the executive can establish and administer courts-martial for cases that arise in the use of military force; (3) Congress can establish courts for the adjudication of cases involving "public rights," such as for the review of agency decisions. Inasmuch as adjudicating contractual rights (the focus of this case) involves the private rights of petitioners, Congress cannot provide for courts on which judges serve for limited terms and under salary restrictions. 458 U.S. 50 (1982), at pp. 64–67.

53. See note 52, particularly on the matter of private versus public rights.

54. For a recent discussion of this, see Louis Fisher, *Constitutional Dialogues* (Princeton: Princeton University Press, 1988), 221–29.

55. Engel v. Vitale, 370 U.S. 421 (1962).

56. 347 U.S. 483 (1954); 349 U.S. 294 (1955).

57. Quoted in Fisher, *Constitutional Dialogues*, 221.

58. Montesquieu argued that "as for the three powers mentioned above [legislative, executive, and judicial], the judicial, in a sense, has no force." Richter, *The Political Theory of Montesquieu*, 249.

59. "Cautionary considerations" are defined by Corwin, "as the desire of the Court to avoid occasions of direct conflict with the political branches of the government, and especially with that branch which wields the physical forces of government, the president." Loss, *Corwin on the Constitution*, 2:196.

60. Justice Stevens wrote in the case of Duke Power Co. v. Carolina Environmental Study Group, 438 U.S. 59, 103 (1978): "We are not statesmen; we are judges. When it is necessary to resolve a constitutional issue in the adjudication of an actual case or controversy, it is our duty to do so. But whenever we are persuaded by reasons of expediency to engage in the business of giving legal advice, we chip away a part of the foundation of our independence and our strength." A number of state courts, however, do issue advisory opinions.

61. In addition, the federal courts can issue "declaratory judgments" in which the courts provide preventive relief in advance of an injury. Declaratory judgments are limited to actual controversies in order to avoid the issuance of advisory opinions. See Fisher, *Constitutional Dialogues*, 93.

62. Baker v. Carr, 369 U.S. 186, 217 (1962).

63. See William O. Douglas, "Stare Decisis," *Columbia Law Review* 49 (1949): 735–58.

64. See Tribe, *American Constitutional Law*, 25; and Chicot County Drainage District v. Baxter State Bank, 308 U.S. 371 (1940). Tribe argues that a finding of unconstitutionality does not invalidate a law. In fact, "if the Supreme Court overrules a prior decision of unconstitutionality, the legislature need not reenact the statute."

65. An important example of a case in which the Court made a ruling that appeared, in the opinion of some, to interfere with the legislative function is the case of Roe v. Wade, 410 U.S. 113 (1973). In that case, Justice Harry Blackmun argued that the "right of privacy" encompasses the right of a woman to have an abortion. Abortion opponents argue that the right of privacy is a wholly judicial construct as interpreted by the Court and that the Court usurped the legislative function when it forbade the states and Congress to determine when and under what conditions an abortion is legal. See Joan Biskupic, "Abortion Protagonists Gird for Crucial Court Test," *Congressional Quarterly Weekly Report* 47 (8 April 1989): 753–58.

66. See Corwin, "Judicial Review in Action," in Loss, *Corwin on the Constitution*, 2:194–217, for a more complete discussion of the use of the "threshold requirements" for judicial review.

67. See Justice Brandeis's concurring opinion in Ashwander v. TVA, 297 U.S. 288, 346–48 (1936).

68. Goldwater v. Carter, 444 U.S. 996 (1979). See also Crockett v. Reagan, 558 F.Supp. 893 (D.D.C. 1982) for the same kind of outcome. The doctrine of standing is particularly important to the determination of whether or not class-action suits are justiciable. For a discussion of this, see Antonin Scalia, "The Doctrine of Standing: An Essential Element of the Separation of Powers," *Suffolk University Law Review* 17 (1983): 881–99.

69. Fisher, *Constitutional Dialogues*, 102; National Organization of Women v. Idaho, 459 U.S. 809 (1982).

70. See Justice Sandra O'Connor's dissenting opinion in Garcia v. San Antonio Metro Transit Authority, 469 U.S. 528, 581 (1985), for a comment on the problems associated with trying to ascertain the framers' intent.

71. See Alexander M. Bickel, *The Least Dangerous Branch* (New York: Bobbs-Merrill, 1962) for a discussion of the weakness of the court; and John Agresto, *The Supreme Court and Constitutional Democracy* (Ithaca: Cornell University Press, 1984) for the obverse argument.

72. See Alexander M. Bickel, *The Least Dangerous Branch*.

73. Wood v. Georgia, 370 U.S. 375, 383 (1962). See also Pennekemp v. Florida, 328 U.S. 331 (1946).

74. Justice Holmes wrote in Schenk v. United States, 249 U.S. 47, 52 (1919): "The question in every case is whether the words used are used in circumstances and are of such a nature as to create a clear and present danger that they will bring about the substantive evils that Congress has a right to prevent." The question in this case related to the constitutional use of speech in contravention to a law (a draft law) passed by Congress. The courts have since expanded the application of the test of a "clear and present danger."

75. 314 U.S. 252, 263 (1941).

76. See also Craig v. Harney, U.S. 367, 376 (1947).

77. "Judges are supposed to be men of fortitude, able to thrive in a hardy climate." Craig v. Harney, ibid., 376.

78. 388 U.S. 307, 321 (1967).

79. Ibid. 315 and 318.

80. See Shuttlesworth v. City of Birmingham, 394 U.S. 147 (1969).

81. On the issue of prior restraint, or the assurance that the state not have the power to suppress, in advance, the publication of materials, see Near v. Minnesota, 283 U.S. 697 (1931); Organization for a Better Austin v. Keefe, 402 U.S. 415 (1971); and *New York Times* v. United States, 403 U.S. 713 (1971), which is better known as the Pentagon Papers case.

82. Nebraska Press Association v. Stuart, 427 U.S. 539 (1976).

83. Lloyd v. Vincent, 423 U.S. 937 (1975).

84. Geise v. United States, 361 U.S. 842 (1959).

6: Prerogative Powers and the Constitution

1. Readers should note the similarity between the arguments made by President Taft (in chapter 3) and Thomas Jefferson's reasoning as well as the simi-

larity between Theodore Roosevelt's position on presidential powers and the case made by Hamilton supporting the constitutionality of the Bank's charter.

2. Thomas Jefferson, quoted in Gunther, *Cases and Materials on Constitutional Law,* 100. This is almost a direct quotation of the Tenth Amendment. It should be noted that Jefferson was a much more enthusiastic supporter of the Bill of Rights than was Hamilton, who was more likely to refer to the main body of the constitutional text. It should also be noted that Jefferson was not so restrictive in his interpretation of the Constitution by the time he became president.

3. Ibid., 100–101.

4. Ibid., 101–3.

5. Hamilton's views in this regard were also the subject of the "Pacificus-Helvidius" debate, which is discussed at length in chapter 3.

6. James D. Richardson, *Messages and Papers of the Presidents* (Washington, D.C.: U.S. GPO, 1896–99), 1:201–2.

7. Ibid., 1:584.

8. Ibid., 2:18.

9. McCulloch v. Maryland, 4 Wheat. 316 (1819).

10. Gibbons v. Ogden, 9 Wheat. 1 (1824).

11. Madison had vetoed similar legislation in 1815 but had noted at that time that the prevailing approval of the Bank superseded his opinions with regard to the constitutionality of the Bank's charter. He therefore opted to waive the question of congressional powers under the "necessary and proper" clause to charter such a bank. *Messages and Papers of the President,* 1:555.

12. McCulloch v. Maryland, 4 Wheat. 316 (1819); see also Osborn v. Bank of the United States, 9 Wheat. 738 (1824).

13. On this point see Charles L. Black, *Structure and Relationship in Constitutional Law* (Woodbridge, Conn.: Ox Bow Press, 1968).

14. The Constitution stipulates that the "necessary and proper" clause appertains to "all other Powers vested by this Constitution in the Government of the United States, or in any Department or Officer thereof." In other words, the "necessary and proper" clause extends to powers and the other branches of government well beyond the enumerated powers provided to Congress under Article 1, sect. 8.

15. Justice Marshall wrote: "Let the end be legitimate, let it be within the scope of the constitution, and all means which are appropriate, which are plainly adapted to that end, which are not prohibited, but consistent with the letter and spirit of the constitution are constitutional." McCulloch v. Maryland, 4 Wheat. 316 (1819), 421.

16. Kinsella v. Singleton, 361 U.S. 234, 247 (1960). Gunther in *Cases and Materials on Constitutional Law* (123), suggests that the Kinsella case is in fact a "belated, albeit limited, victory for the position repudiated by Marshall."

17. Charles Howard McIlwain, *Constitutionalism: Ancient and Modern* (Ithaca: Cornell University Press, 1940), 32.

18. On this point see also Agresto, *The Supreme Court and Constitutional Democracy,* 53.

19. Madison was very explicit in *Federalist* paper 10 that the Constitution created a "republic," which, at the time, had a meaning quite distinct from a democracy. *Federalist Papers,* 81.

20. Clinton Rossiter, *Constitutional Dictatorship* (Princeton: Princeton University Press, 1948), 212.

21. Locke, *Second Treatise*, 84.

22. Sotirios Barber, *On What the Constitution Means* (Baltimore: Johns Hopkins University Press, 1984), chap. 6.

23. Richardson, *Messages and Papers of the Presidents*, 6:24.

24. Barber, *On What the Constitution Means*, 189.

25. Ibid.

26. Ibid., 190.

27. Prize Cases, 2 Black (67 U.S.) 635, 668 (1862).

28. Barber, *On What the Constitution Means*, 83.

29. As Hamilton argued in *Federalist* paper 28: "[I]f the representatives of the people betray their constituents, there is then no resource left but in the exertion of that original right of self-defense which is paramount to all positive forms of government." *Federalist Papers*, 180.

30. The president, with substantial powers and resources at his disposal, is hardly in a defensive position. Citizens who have been victimized by the state, in exercising their right of self-defense, do not have access to coercive forces of the state and the publicity focus of the presidency. The right of self-defense in the Lockean analysis is clearly exercised by the citizen against a renegade ruler. However, the *prerogative* power, according to Locke, is to be exercised by the *ruler* in pursuit of the public good. To suggest, as Barber does, that the exercise of presidential prerogative is not the exercise of power by a ruler is not only unfaithful to the Lockean construct but is also an unjustified exercise in semantics. Lincoln was a "ruler" whether or not he was acting as president.

31. Arthur S. Miller, "Toward a Definition of 'The' Constitution," repr. in his *Politics, Democracy, and the Supreme Court*, 19–101. I apologize to the author of this article for the superficiality of my description of his thoughts. The essence of the argument, however, is preserved.

32. Ibid., 51.

33. Ibid., 49–50.

34. For a much less radical rendition of this same argument, see Fisher, *Constitutional Dialogues*, 275. He writes: "What is 'final' at one stage of our political development may be reopened at some later date, leading to revisions, fresh interpretations, and reversals of Court doctrines. Through this process of interaction among the branches, all three institutions are able to expose weaknesses, hold excesses in check, and gradually forge a consensus on constitutional issues."

35. See John Hart Ely, *Democracy and Distrust: A Theory of Judicial Review* (Cambridge: Harvard University Press, 1980), 1.

36. Ibid.

37. See Robert A. Dahl, "A Critique of the Ruling Elite Model," *American Political Science Review* 58 (1958): 369–463, for a classic critique of elite theory. See also Mancur Olson, *The Logic of Collective Action: Public Goods and the Theory of Groups* (New York: Schocken Books, 1968), for a discussion of the nature and sources of class bias in political decision making.

38. Barber, *On What the Constitution Means*, 188–96.

39. See Samuel Huntington, *Political Order in Changing Societies* (New Haven: Yale University Press, 1968), 1–95. Effective political systems are charac-

terized by "strong, adaptable, coherent political institutions" including effective bureaucracies, popular participation, and procedures for regulating succession.

40. Ely, *Democracy and Distrust,* 92.

41. Ely, ibid., 87, bases his argument on the assumption that the Constitution is not "an enduring but evolving statement of general values"; instead, the Constitution enshrines a set of governing procedures.

42. See *Democracy and Distrust,* 77–88, for Ely's discussion of the meaning and purpose of representative government.

43. Ibid., 100–101.

44. See Jefferson's letter to John Breckenridge, quoted in chapter 3.

45. The standing investigatory committees of Congress, which so actively inquired into President Lincoln's conduct of the war, were one of the permanent fixtures of Congress created by the Civil War. In addition, Justice Taney ordered the release of one John Merryman of Baltimore, who was being held under President Lincoln's suspension of the writ by the commander of the military forces in the area. Merryman was eventually handed over to civilian authorities. See *Ex parte* Merryman, 17 Fed. Cases 144 (1861).

46. On 7 September 1942 Roosevelt said in an address to Congress:

I ask the Congress to take this action [repealing certain provisions of the Price Control Act] by the first of October. Inaction on your part by that date will leave me with an inescapable responsibility to the people of this country to see to it that the war effort is no longer imperiled by threat of economic chaos.
   In the event that the Congress should fail to act, and act adequately, I shall accept the responsibility, and I will act.

New York Times, 8 September 1942, quoted in Corwin, *The President,* 250.

47. There is some evidence to suggest that this notion of constitutionalism is as old as the ancient Greeks and Romans. See McIlwain, *Constitutionalism,* 27–28.

48. Although I disagree with some of their conclusions, I find the best illustration that political order is a function of a widely shared political culture in Gabriel Almond and Sidney Verba, *The Civic Culture* (Princeton: Princeton University Press, 1963); see also Gabriel Almond and Sidney Verba, eds., *The Civic Culture Revisited* (Boston: Little, Brown, 1980).

49. Story, *Commentaries on the Constitution of the United States,* 174–75, n.1.

50. See Hamilton, Federalist paper 84. *Federalist Papers,* 510–20.

51. Washington wrote that "a primary object of such a national institution [a national university] should be the education of our youth in the science of government. *Messages and Papers of the Presidents,* 1:202.

52. Jefferson in a letter to Fitzhugh, 1798 quoted in Padover, *Thomas Jefferson on Democracy,* 52.

53. Hamilton, *Federalist* paper 9. *Federalist Papers,* 72.

54. In *Democracy in America* (New York: Doubleday, 1969), Alexis de Tocqueville wrote, "In America the purely practical side of science is cultivated admirably, and trouble is taken about the theoretical side immediately necessary to application. On this side the Americans always display a clear, free, original, and creative turn of mind. But hardly anyone in the United States devotes himself to the essentially theoretical and abstract side of human knowledge" (460). Americans still have more faith in science than do citizens of other nations. In

a recent poll, 58 percent of Americans were reported to believe that "science will help mankind," while only 35 percent of Europeans hold the same belief. See Ben J. Wattenberg, "The Attitudes Behind American Exceptionalism," *US News and World Report* 107 (7 August 1989): 25.

55. On this point see Sidney Verba and Gary R. Orren, *Equality in America: The View from the Top* (Cambridge: Harvard University Press, 1985).

56. What, exactly, is the "elite" philosophy and who is this "elite"?

57. The exceptions to which I refer are elaborated upon in chapters 2–4. For example, in extraordinary situations, the president exercises prerogative powers that violate the rights of individuals, even in peacetime. Congress can subpoena and compel individuals to testify under the threat of a contempt of Congress citation. The courts can silence press coverage of court proceedings in select cases.

58. 1 U.S.C. 112b.

59. Congressional leaders were not informed about the rescue mission until after the mission failed and the military contingent was being withdrawn.

60. Youngstown Co. v. Sawyer 343 U.S. 579, 662 (1952).

61. For a defense of the position that oversight of government activities is best left to the "market," see Matthew D. McCubbins and Thomas Schwartz, "Congressional Oversight Overlooked: Police Patrols Versus Fire Alarms," *American Journal of Political Science* 28 (February 1984): 165–79.

62. *Ex parte* Merryman, 17 Fed. Cases 144 (1861).

63. On 4 April 1864, Abraham Lincoln wrote that "measures otherwise unconstitutional, might become lawful, by becoming indispensable to the preservation of the nation." John Nicolay and John Hay, eds., *The Complete Works of Abraham Lincoln* (New York: Century, 1894), 10:66; quoted in Barber, *On What the Constitution Means*, 190.

Index

Adams, John Quincy, 100, 121; administration of, 102, 103
Administrative Procedures Act (1946), 65
Advisory opinions, 109–10, 160n.60
Amendments to the Constitution, 10; Equal Rights, 113; Hughes-Ryan Amendment, 86; First, 51, 76, 77, 114, 115, 135; Fifth, 53, 59, 76, 77, 80, 131; Sixth, 53, 59, 115, 131; Tenth, 162n.2; Eleventh, 102, 105, 106; Thirteenth, 106; Fourteenth, 106, 131; Fifteenth, 106; Sixteenth, 106; Twenty-Second, 147n.9; Twenty-Sixth, 106
American Constitution, the: Article 1, 48, 59–60, 71; Article 1, section 7, 154n.28; Article 1, section 8, 118, 120, 122, 162n.14; Article 1, section 9, 118, 125; Article 2, 47, 48, 71, 95; Article 3, 95, 99, 108, 159n.41, 159n.52; Article 6, clause 2, 157n.19; commander in chief clause in, 53–54, 72; and Congress, 39, 71, 72, 73, 74, 80–81, 101, 103, 106; contractual components of, 16, 34, 91, 129–30; courts and, 72–73, 92, 98, 99, 100, 106, 111–12; and English Constitution, 11, 12, 16; and the executive, 8, 19, 31, 32, 36, 39, 71; interpretation of, 34, 47, 48, 66–67, 72–73, 89, 104, 109, 126–28, 152n.1, 164n.41; and the judiciary, 39, 99–100, 115, 157n.16; and the legislative, 36, 39, 71–74; necessary and proper clause of, 117–

18, 119–20, 121, 122–23, 162n.11, n.14; and president, 66–67, 71; as process, 15, 131–32, 136, 137. *See also* Amendments to the Constitution; Articles of Confederation; Bill of Rights; Constitutional Convention
American Revolution, the, 10, 18, 28, 30, 31, 32, 36, 38; time of, 19, 24, 29, 35, 92–93. *See also* Framers of the Constitution
Aquinas, Thomas, 145n.19
Aristotle, 145n.19
Articles of Confederation, 19, 31–32, 36, 39; and legislatures, 94, 95, 99, 102, 130, 145n.28

Bacon, Francis, 21
Bagehot, Walter, 12, 90
Baker, James, 154n.31
Baker v. Carr case, 110–11
Bank of the United States, 118–19, 121, 122, 162n.11
Bankruptcy Act (1978), 108
Barber, Sotirios, 124–26, 129, 163n.30
Barenblatt, Lloyd, 77
Barnes, Michael, 61
Barton, Bruce, 55
Belmont, August, 58
Bill of Rights, 39, 42; and Congress, 75, 90, 159n.46; and Constitution, 37–38, 131, 147n.44, 158n.21, 162n.2; in emergencies, 6, 81, 83; interpretation of, 72–73, 132; and liberties, 10, 15, 133, 137; and prerogative powers, 45, 48, 51, 52, 68, 123; violated, 123, 124

Dred Scott decision, 105, 106
Duane, James, 35

Eliot, Sir John, 24, 144n.12
Ellsworth, Justice Oliver, 100
Ely, John Hart, 128, 129, 134
Emergency, 48, 142n.10; and Bill of
  Rights, 6, 81, 83; and Congress, 54–
  55, 56, 70–71, 72, 79, 83, 84, 135–
  36, 137; and courts, 12, 135–36,
  137; president and, 55, 56, 67–68,
  135–36; what constitutes, 7, 8, 42–
  43, 54, 55, 67, 82–83. *See also*
  Emergency powers; National Emergency Act (1976)
Emergency Court of Appeal, 80
Emergency powers, 10, 12–13, 14, 15,
  33; of president, 41–42, 50, 54, 57,
  67–68; provision for, 17, 18, 28
Emergency Price Control Act (1942),
  66, 80, 108, 164n.46
English Constitution, the, 4, 11, 12, 16
Enlightenment thinking, 11, 15, 20–21,
  37
Equal Rights Amendment, 113
Executive, the, 8, 9, 33, 45, 83, 85–86,
  99, 145n.27; Congress and, 35, 36,
  37, 61, 63, 64–65, 79, 87, 90,
  151n.53, 159n.52; and the Constitution, 19, 31, 32, 36, 41, 47, 63; and
  foreign affairs, 35, 57, 88–89; and
  funds, 35, 150n.53; and judiciary,
  94, 98–99; and legislature, 17, 36–
  37, 47, 48, 61, 62, 84; Locke and,
  28, 29, 41–42; and prerogative powers, 72, 73; and president, 64–65,
  68–69; and war, 35, 51, 149n.27
Executive agreements, 58–59, 69, 133
Executive Office of the President
  (EOP), 65, 151n.65
Ex parte Milligan, 50–51, 148n.21
Ex parte Quirin, 53
Ex parte Vallandigham, 148n.21

Family Practice of Medicine Act, 60
Federal Register, 63, 65, 68, 151n.58
Filmer, Sir Robert, 23, 144n.10, n.15
Ford, Gerald, 79; administration of, 61
Foreign affairs, 7, 64, 145n.29; and
  Congress, 57, 71, 84, 87–89,
  153n.14, 155n.39; executive and,
  35, 57, 88–89; president's preroga-

tives in, 56–58, 64, 68
Fort Sumter, 13, 49
Framers of the Constitution, 14, 15,
  18–20, 39, 90, 91, 104, 130, 131,
  137; and executive, 32, 36, 41; and
  judiciary, 36, 99, 113, 115; and legislature, 36, 96–97; and prerogative
  powers, 34, 69; and representation,
  43, 44
Freedom of Information Act, 52
French Revolution, the, 158n.30

George III (king), 29, 38, 93, 130,
  145n.25
Georgia House of Representatives, 102
Gibbons v. Ogden case, 121
Glorious Revolution, the, 20, 22, 24,
  38, 93, 94
Goldwater v. Carter case, 112–13
Gorham, Nathaniel, 99, 101
Grenada, 58
Grier, Justice, 50
Gulf of Tonkin Resolution, 135

Hamilton, Alexander, 131, 146n.41,
  147n.5, 162n.2; and Bank of the
  United States, 118, 119, 122,
  162n.1; and executive, 36–37, 45,
  147n.8; and judiciary, 36–37, 92,
  100, 157n.15, 158n.21; as "Pacifi-
  cus," 47, 48, 162n.5; and presi-
  dency, 45–46, 146n.43
Hamilton v. Kentucky Distilleries Co.
  case, 149n.31
Harlan, Justice, 77, 149n.22
Hobbes, Thomas, 26, 27
Holmes, Justice, 81, 109
Home Building and Loan Association,
  82; v. Blaisdell case, 128–29
House of Commons, 23, 30, 38, 93
House of Representatives, 61, 78, 85,
  89, 105; Committee on Un-American
  Activities, 76, 77
Housing and Rent Act (1947), 54
Hughes, Justice Charles Evans, 82–83,
  109, 128–29
Hughes-Ryan Amendment, 86
Hume, David, 19, 144n.14
Huntington, Samuel, 127–28

Immigration and Naturalization Act,
  85

Pitt Series in Policy and Institutional Studies
Bert A. Rockman, Editor

"He Shall Not Pass This Way Again": The Legacy of Justice William O. Douglas
Stephen L. Wasby, Editor

Homeward Bound: Explaining Changes in Congressional Behavior
Glenn Parker

How Does Social Science Work? Reflections on Practice
Paul Diesing

Imagery and Ideology in U.S. Policy Toward Libya, 1969–1982
Mahmoud G. ElWarfally

The Impact of Policy Analysis
James M. Rogers

Iran and the United States: A Cold War Case Study
Richard W. Cottam

Japanese Prefectures and Policymaking
Steven R. Reed

Making Regulatory Policy
Keith Hawkins and John M. Thomas, Editors

Managing the Presidency: Carter, Reagan, and the Search for Executive Harmony
Colin Campbell, S.J.

Organizing Governance, Governing Organizations
Colin Campbell, S.J., and B. Guy Peters, Editors

Party Organizations in American Politics
Cornelius P. Cotter et al.

Perceptions and Behavior in Soviet Foreign Policy
Richard K. Herrmann

Pesticides and Politics: The Life Cycle of a Public Issue
Christopher J. Bosso

Policy Analysis by Design
Davis B. Bobrow and John S. Dryzek

The Political Failure of Employment Policy, 1945–1982
Gary Mucciaroni

Political Leadership: A Source Book
Barbara Kellerman, Editor

The Politics of Public Utility Regulation
William T. Gormley, Jr.

The Politics of the U.S. Cabinet: Representation in the Executive Branch, 1789–1984
Jeffrey E. Cohen